COUNTRY SUPPERS
from Uphill Farm

Library of Congress
Cataloging-in-Publication Data

    Lowe-Clay, Carol.
       Country suppers from Uphill Farm /
    by Carol Lowe-Clay.
       p.   cm.
    Includes index.
    ISBN 0–913589–74–8
    1. Cookery, American. 2. Country life—
       Vermont.   I. Title.
    TX715.L9103 1993
    641.5973—dc20   93–1527
                       CIP

Photographs: Becky Luigart–Stayner
Printing: Capital City Press

Williamson Publishing Co.
P.O. Box 185
Charlotte, Vermont 05445
800-234-7891

Manufactured in the United States of America

10 9 8 7 6 5 4 3 2 1

Portions of this book previously appeared in
Carol Lowe-Clay's *Simply Elegant Country
Foods*.

To O: For then and for now.

*I am grateful for the time spent at Uphill
Farm. It changed my life. The memories are
rich. Many people made the place work and
share a love for that time: Ann, George, Elly,
Sarah, Abby, Clem, Kate, Lang, Owen, Jay,
Harold, and the memory of Mrs. Mattison. In
different ways, Uphill Farm was home to
each of us.*

*And thanks to Jenn for her idea and for
sticking with it.*

COUNTRY SUPPERS
from Uphill Farm

Carol Lowe-Clay

WILLIAMSON PUBLISHING • CHARLOTTE, VERMONT 05445

COUNTRY SUPPERS
from Uphill Farm

At Uphill Farm • 6

Around the Meal • 12

Chicken & Asparagus Soup
Summer Gazpacho
Sweet & Sour Cabbage Soup
Roasted Eggplant & Tomato Bisque
Butternut Squash Bisque
Baked Red Onion & Garlic Soup Au Gratin
Vermont Cheese Soup with
  Herbed Croutons
Black Bean Soup
Uphill Farm Antipasto Platter:
  Whole Roasted Garlic
  Baked Chèvre
  Red Pepper Marmalade
Aubergine Spread
Whole Wheat Blueberry Muffins
Sarah's Pumpkin Bread
Catharine's Oatmeal & Molasses Bread
Sweet Cream Scones

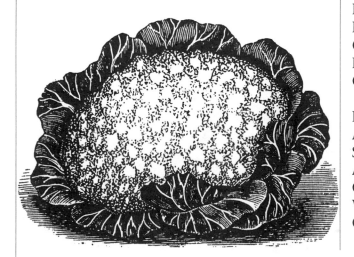

Seasonal Salads • 28

Broccoli & Pasta Salad with
  Sun-dried Tomato Vinaigrette
Marinated Asparagus
Chicken & Orzo Salad
Hungarian Rice Salad
Shrimp & Potato Salad
Chicken & Greens with Orange Vinaigrette
Green Bean & New Potato Salad
Braised Leeks in Crème Fraîche
Red Cabbage & Blue Cheese Salad
Lentil & Brown Rice Salad
Marinated Chick Pea Salad
Salad Dressings:
  Favorite Vinaigrette
  In-the-Bowl Dressing
  Lemon-Dijon Dressing
  Honey-Soy Vinaigrette
  Sour Cream Dressing
  Warm Bacon Dressing

Glorious Vegetables • 44

Spicy Stewed Eggplant
Brigitte's Onion Tart
Fried Green Tomatoes
On-the-Grill Vegetables
Buttery Baked Corn
Green Beans, Potatoes, &
  Cornmeal Dumplings
Lacy Leek & Potato Cakes
Artichoke Risotto
Sauerkraut & Apples
A Galaxy of Onions
Golden Potato Puree
Wintry Potato Casserole
Ginger & Garlic Winter Squash

At Uphill Farm

I first went to Uphill Farm in 1974. I went because Owen was there. It was fall — apple season. The orchard, set on the hillside of Mt. Equinox, framed a spectacular view of the Battenkill River Valley. The white farmhouse where he lived stood surrounded by a stonewall and a garden wild with hydrangea, iris, and pasture roses. Across the way was a large red barn and its pasture, where Jersey cows and sheep often watched us work. And from the field, the white steeple of the church, where we were later married, was visible.

Each year, the apple harvesting lasted for weeks. The orchard was full with people balanced on ladders, bags strapped across their chests, reaching into the branches for fruit. Full baskets of apples were loaded into the truck and driven to the barn, where a huge hydraulic apple press waited. Gallons and gallons of the absolute best cider I've ever tasted were bottled. Indoors perfect apples were wrapped in newspaper and stored in the cellar. Apples were sliced and dried on screens over the wood stove. They were frozen into pie shapes, canned and frozen, and made into sauces and spicy butter.

That fall was the beginning of a whole new awareness for me. The focus on seasonal work and daily chores cycled in both an immediate and a timeless way, connecting me to people who worried over rain or a fox in the barnyard a hundred years before. Older wisdom fueled it all. Jay and Harold, two brothers who were raised on the hill, now came up from town. They brought stories, a sense of history, and taught us woodchuck cures and garden tips. They hunted and trapped in the woods, helped with sugaring, and talked us through "how it was."

I stayed on there, longer and longer, through all the seasons. I learned secrets. The pork was so delicious because Owen's pigs ate week-old English muffins and raisin bread dropped off by the Pepperidge Farm delivery man. And the turkeys followed him everywhere; they strutted and preened for him. He raised them from chicks in the living room and they really did love him. Classical music played in the barn during morning milking as daylight came over the mountain.

Owen stayed at Uphill year-round. His brothers and sisters stayed whenever they could, often bringing friends home from school, Europe, "the city." There was terrific energy as farming activity combined a reverence for the past with the spiritedness of new possibilities. There were always plenty of

people around, helping with fencing, haying, or sugaring. Everyone wanted to be a part of the place, even if to just drink tea, play boules, or hang around.

Uphill Farm was not fancy, but comfortable with a style all its own. That style was a good representation of what our lives were like then. We lived simply, trying to take care of, as well as live off the land. Mrs. Mattison, the previous owner, had farmed and raised her family there. Evidence of her life was everywhere, mingled together with what we brought to the place. Her old calendars from the local feed store remained, as did her postcard collection amid our poker chips and board games. Julia Child and Elizabeth David cooking books joined her copies of church supper and grange cookbooks — we used them all. We loved and took care of her gardens, but made them our own, too. Shallots, leeks, and French tarragon were planted beside her rhubarb.

The house, built in 1790, was rambling — small rooms off other small rooms. It was drafty, uninsulated — sometimes cold. On the coldest nights, we would move downstairs and sleep around the wood stove. It was cozy, wintry, alive to the season. Seasonal work brought seasonal rewards. Food was grown, raised, or produced. In the stone cellar, we stored canned tomatoes and other fruits and vegetables, on the

shelves. Bushels of Seckel pears and apples lined the walls. There was always a pitcher of spoonably thick top milk in the refrigerator. Garlic and onions were braided and hung in the larder. And butter and eggs were always fresh and in abundance as well.

This abundance usually seemed a gift but was sometimes a challenge. Meals were planned according to what was ready to be picked or what was overfilling the freezer — and how exactly to cook it was the challenge. I was learning how to cook at the time. Enthusiasm was sometimes greater than skill. Owen's mother, Ann, and inspiring cook, lived down the road at Wild Farm. She leant us books: **Gourmet Vols. I & II, Mastering the Art of French Cooking**, and **The Joy of Cooking**. Learning classic cooking techniques allowed me to practice one recipe with varying ingredients. I experimented with cream soups using leeks, watercress, peas, or sorrel. I practiced ragouts, omelets, and soufflés. Incorporating bits of vegetable or leftover ingredients into meal planning made me feel like a true country cook. I tried not to waste anything.

Simple techniques such as making a pie crust or folding egg whites into cakes were new and fun. Cooking became an adventure and was no longer scary. I read lots of cookbooks, wrote notes and drew in the margins. I kept seasonal recipe files. It was all a great pleasure.

I learned to see meals relative to the gardening cycle and its changing bounty. Garden-based meals have great versatility. A late summer dinner might include roasted eggplant soup, an herb omelet, and green salad vinaigrette. A few weeks later as my garden became plentiful with autumn vegetables, the menu might be poule au pot and pears in crème caramel.

For this book, I've taken the best of what I learned along the way and developed them in new ways, sometimes using lower fat alternatives in place of traditionally richer preparations. But there are some recipes that I choose to leave unaltered, in part because of sentiment, partly because alternatives lack in flavor.

Though we live somewhere else now, the experiences and influences of Uphill Farm continue to affect the way I cook and live. Gathering together in the evening continues to be a favorite time for me and my family. The simple pleasure of good food, good wine, and good friends enrich us. Memories of nights at Uphill Farm stay with me — the peaceful feeling as night darkened the hillside, Mt. Equinox looming vast above us, and the warmth of the wood stove and friendships drew us in closer together. I feel that closeness still.

AROUND THE MEAL

Chicken & Asparagus Soup

Summer Gazpacho

Sweet & Sour Cabbage Soup

Roasted Eggplant & Tomato Bisque

Butternut Squash Bisque

Baked Red Onion & Garlic Soup Au Gratin

Vermont Cheese Soup with Herbed Croutons

Black Bean Soup

Uphill Farm Antipasto Platter:
Whole Roasted Garlic
Baked Chèvre
Red Pepper Marmalade

Aubergine Spread

Whole Wheat Blueberry Muffins

Sarah's Pumpkin Bread

Catharine's Oatmeal & Molasses Bread

Sweet Cream Scones

CHICKEN & ASPARAGUS SOUP

Most years we get some snow in April, but it still catches us by surprise. One April day we were planting onion sets, and the next day we were totally snowed in. The town plow couldn't get through up the hill. Neighbors snow-shoed over to share in this unexpected holiday. I made this soup and we enjoyed the irony of spring asparagus and spring snow. It was a cozy sort of storm.

One 3-pound whole chicken, or 2 whole chicken breasts

1–2 cups mixed vegetables (celery tops, garlic, onion, carrots)

1 ounce dried porcini mushrooms

1 small bunch asparagus, about 2 cups, cleaned and sliced in 1" pieces

1/2 lemon

1 onion

3 cloves garlic

1/4 cup olive oil

3–4 cups water

1 tablespoon flour

1/2 cup white wine

1. To cook chicken and prepare broth: Cover chicken with cold water. Add any leftover broth, wine, or cider if available. Scatter vegetables over and simmer until chicken is done, about 30 minutes (for breasts) to 45 minutes (for a whole chicken). Remove chicken from pot, remove meat from bones, and set aside. Return bones and skin to soup pot; add enough water to yield 4 cups broth, and continue to simmer for 1 hour. Strain and cool broth. If there is time, chill broth to allow fat to rise and harden. Remove and discard fat.

2. Soak mushrooms in 1 cup hot water until soft. Remove mushrooms and set aside. Reserve water.

3. Squeeze juice of lemon over sliced asparagus.

4. Mince together mushrooms, onion, and garlic.

5. In a soup pot, saute the mushroom mixture in olive oil until softened.

6. Add 4 cups chicken broth. Pour in mushroom-soaking liquid; be careful to leave out grit on bottom.

7. Bring to a simmer. Add asparagus and simmer 5 minutes longer.

8. Mix flour with white wine. Stir into soup.

9. Add chicken to soup, simmering 10 minutes more.

YIELD: 6–8 servings
PREPARATION TIME: 1 hour
COOKING TIME: 2 hours

Summer Gazpacho

Gazpacho is a favorite summer soup, reflecting the abundance of our garden. One memorable, hot, late summer day, a small group of us went walking into the sugar woods. Owen had baby Slater in a frontpack and a wildly impractical lunch in a basket backpack. Icy gazpacho filled a ½ gallon Mason jar, and wine glasses wrapped in cloth napkins were packed to serve it in. For dessert, we carried rich chocolate mousse and thick Jersey cream. We even brought a rotary beater and bowl to whip it in. As Slater slept, we enjoyed our meal and the quiet shade of the maple woods.

2 medium-sized cucumbers

1 green pepper, seeded and chopped

1 small red onion, finely chopped

3 tomatoes, peeled, seeded, and diced

4 cups tomato juice

3 tablespoons olive oil or vegetable oil

2 tablespoons wine vinegar

3–4 fresh basil leaves, snipped

½ avocado, optional

Salt and pepper

Sour cream or yogurt, optional

Pea pods or zucchini for garnish

Optional garnishes

1. Prepare the vegetables in a food processor (if one is available), one vegetable at a time, taking care *not* to puree any of the vegetables.

2. Peel cucumber and cut in half lengthwise. If seeds are large, scoop out with a spoon and discard.

3. Chop cucumber, then place in a large bowl with green pepper, onion, tomatoes, tomato juice, oil, wine vinegar, and basil leaves.

4. Peel optional avocado, cut into 1" cubes, and stir into gazpacho.

5. Add salt and pepper to taste. Cover and chill for at least 2 hours.

6. To serve, ladle into soup bowls, and top with a dollop of sour cream or yogurt, if desired. Garnish with four pea pods arranged like wheel spokes. Pass bowls of homemade croutons, thinly sliced zucchini, black olives, and cubes of cucumber.

YIELD: 6 servings
PREPARATION TIME: 20 minutes

SWEET & SOUR CABBAGE SOUP

Cabbages planted early in the season survive the May frosts common in Vermont. We planted a lot of them, since by May we couldn't wait to get our hands into the ground and because they stored well. This soup is a terrific use for cabbage. Like many hearty soups, it benefits from a slow simmer and from being made at least a day in advance.

1½ **pounds fresh brisket or chuck steak, trimmed of fat and cut into thin strips**

2 **tablespoons butter or margarine**

1 **head cabbage, cut into 1" pieces or coarsely shredded**

1 **large onion, chopped**

1 **(8-ounce) can tomato sauce**

½ **cup canned tomatoes, drained and chopped**

3 **tablespoons brown sugar**

2 **tablespoons lemon juice**

2 **teaspoons paprika**

2 **cups carrots, coarsely grated**

1 **teaspoon salt**

7 **cups water**

½ **teaspoon sour salt (also known as citric acid), optional**

1. Melt butter or margarine over high heat in a 5-quart soup pot.

2. Add meat, cabbage, and onion, and cook for 15 minutes. Stir often, until the cabbage is tender.

3. Add tomato sauce, tomatoes, brown sugar, lemon juice, paprika, salt, and water.

4. Bring to a boil; then cover and simmer for 1 hour.

5. Add the carrots; simmer for an additional 30 minutes.

6. Stir in the optional sour salt.

YIELD: 8 servings
PREPARATION TIME: 25 minutes
COOKING TIME: 1 hour 45 minutes

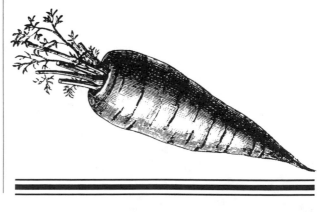

Roasted Eggplant & Tomato Bisque

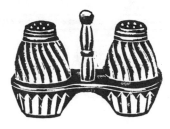

Eggplants love heat and long growing seasons. At Uphill, we were short of both. Eggplants, like tomatoes, ripen late in the season and are often ready to be picked at the same time. This late summer soup combines the flavors of both for a savory soup.

1 large eggplant

1 tablespoon butter or margarine

1 tablespoon olive oil

2 cloves garlic, minced

1 medium onion, chopped fine

1 small carrot, chopped

5 ripe tomatoes, peeled, or 3 – 3 1/2 cups canned tomatoes

3 cups chicken or vegetable broth, or 2 (14-ounce) cans broth

1/4 cup half-and-half or light cream, optional

Salt and pepper

1. Preheat oven to 350 degrees.

2. Prick eggplant with fork and bake for 60–70 minutes. Allow to cool.

3. Heat butter and oil in a soup pot. Cook garlic, onion, and carrot slowly for 5 minutes. Do not brown.

4. Add tomatoes and broth. Cook over medium heat for 1 1/2 hours.

5. Cut open eggplant. Skin will easily peel away. Chop coarsely.

6. Add eggplant to soup. Cook 5 minutes more.

7. Let soup cool for a few minutes and puree in a blender in 2 batches, until smooth.

8. Thin with additional broth, if necessary.

9. Reheat, stir in optional half-and-half, and season with salt and pepper.

YIELD: 4 servings
PREPARATION TIME: 10 minutes
COOKING TIME: 2 1/2 hours

BUTTERNUT SQUASH BISQUE

Squash soup was a sure sign of late October. Perhaps this is because it has the same fading gold color as the fields. The crisp tartness of new apples and the mellow richness of squash are a wonderful fall combination, as this soup proves.

1 small butternut squash, about 1 – 1¼ pounds

2 green apples, peeled, cored, and coarsely chopped

1 small onion, chopped

¼ – ½ teaspoon curry powder

6 cups rich chicken stock or broth

2 slices bread, cubed

1 teaspoon salt

¼ teaspoon pepper

¼ cup half-and-half

1. Halve and seed the squash.

2. Put the squash, along with the remaining ingredients, except the half-and-half, in a large soup pot.

3. Simmer for 45 minutes.

4. Remove squash. Separate the peel from the squash and return squash to the pot.

5. Puree in a blender or food processor.

6. Reheat the puree; add half-and-half. Heat; do not boil.

7. Serve piping hot in warm bowls.

YIELD: 4–6 servings

PREPARATION TIME: 10 minutes

COOKING TIME: 50 minutes

VARIATION: The half-and-half can be omitted altogether for a lovely, yet lighter, soup.

BAKED RED ONION & GARLIC SOUP AU GRATIN

We loved growing onions and garlic, and especially enjoyed braiding their stems. In early August, the porch was covered with fragrant onions drying on newspapers in the sun. After a few days, I'd braid the stems — a quiet, unhurried time. When I could bear cutting into the braids, I'd make this soup, always welcome on cooler days.

4 medium-sized red onions, thinly sliced

3 cloves garlic, chopped (or less if you prefer a milder garlic taste)

3 tablespoons butter or margarine

2 tablespoons olive oil

1/2 teaspoon salt

1 teaspoon granulated sugar

3 tablespoons flour

9 cups beef, chicken, or vegetable stock (a good canned broth will do)

3/4 cup dry vermouth or white wine

3 tablespoons Cognac or brandy

Slices of French bread

1 1/2 cups grated cheese, Swiss or cheddar

1/3 cup grated hard cheese, Parmesan or Romano

Freshly ground black pepper

1. In a Dutch oven, combine onions and garlic together in the butter and oil. Cover and cook over low heat 15 minutes, until onions are translucent.

2. Stir in the salt and sugar; raise heat to medium.

3. Stir frequently until onions are a deep brown. This will take 30–35 minutes. Keep stirring to prevent burning.

4. Sprinkle flour over onions, stirring for a few minutes.

5. Add broth and vermouth; bring to a boil. Simmer over low heat for half an hour.

6. Stir in Cognac or brandy.

7. Heat slices of French bread in a low oven for 5 minutes.

8. Place bread slices in oven-proof bowls. Ladle soup over bread. Bread will float to the top.

9. Top bread with cheeses. Grind on pepper.

10. Bake in 400 degree oven, until soup is bubbly and top is brown, 20–30 minutes. Serve immediately.

YIELD: 4–6 servings
COOKING TIME: 1 1/2 hours
BAKING TIME: 30 minutes

VERMONT CHEESE SOUP WITH HERBED CROUTONS

We are partial to a good farmhouse cheddar. Cheese soup always seems just right — easy and warming on a wintry night.

Sharp cheeses (aged) melt better in cooking; younger cheeses become gummy. Remember to warm soup bowls before filling, and garnish generously with Herbed Croutons or topping of your choice.

2 tablespoons butter or margarine

2 tablespoons finely chopped onion

1 clove garlic, minced

2 tablespoons flour

1 cup chicken or vegetable broth

5 cups milk

2 cups grated, aged cheddar cheese, packed tightly

1/2 teaspoon Worcestershire sauce

Pinch dry mustard

Salt and pepper

Paprika

Optional garnishes

1. Melt butter or margarine in a soup pot. Add onion and garlic, stirring until golden.

2. Add flour; whisk for a minute or two.

3. Slowly pour in the broth, and then milk. Continue stirring until slightly thickened.

4. Add cheese, Worcestershire sauce, and mustard, stirring in one direction.

5. When cheese is melted, season with salt and pepper.

6. Ladle into heated bowls, sprinkle paprika over each serving, and garnish with the topping of your choice.

YIELD: 4 servings

PREPARATION TIME: 15 minutes

COOKING TIME: 15 minutes

VARIATIONS: Try substituting tomato juice or low-fat milk for broth. Garnishes are limited only by imagination: try popcorn, crumbled bacon, herbed croutons, red peppers, toasted almonds, tomato slices, broccoli pieces, or fresh basil leaves.

HERBED CROUTONS

Herbed croutons are delicious when prepared with a variety of breads and herbs. Cube stale bread; saute quickly in butter or margarine flavored with garlic and herbs. Store in tightly closed jars in the refrigerator.

Croutons can also be prepared by drying bread cubes in a 350 degree oven for 5 minutes. Toss with melted butter or olive oil that has been flavored with garlic and herbs. Continue baking until bread cubes are dried and golden brown, about 3 minutes more.

BLACK BEAN SOUP

In midwinter, when fresh garden meals are past and the larder seems over-stocked with dried beans, potatoes, and onions, this simple soup was a welcome change. Leave plenty of time for the long simmer, essential to its success.

3 tablespoons olive oil

1 small clove garlic, minced

1 onion, finely chopped

1 rib celery, finely chopped

1¹/₂ cups black beans, washed and picked through

6 cups chicken or vegetable broth

Salt and pepper

2 tablespoons chopped parsley

1 tablespoon lemon juice

2 tablespoons sherry

Optional garnishes

1. Heat oil in a soup pot, and gently saute garlic, onion, and celery until tender.

2. Add broth and beans. Bring to a boil, cover, and simmer over low heat for 3 hours.

3. Whirl soup in a food processor or blender, along with salt, pepper, and parsley. This will take a few batches. Return puree to the soup pot.

4. Add lemon juice and sherry. Reheat soup. Adjust consistency by adding more broth if needed (this is usually served as a rather thick soup).

5. Ladle hot soup into warmed soup bowls. Garnish by floating lemon slices with a sprinkling of parsley in each bowl or with a dollop of yogurt and parsley. Finely chopped hard-boiled egg can also be used as the garnish.

YIELD: 6 servings
PREPARATION TIME: 20 minutes
COOKING TIME: 3 hours

Uphill Farm Antipasto Platter

Garlic lovers will happily squeeze this soft, roasted garlic on crusty French bread. The warm Baked Chèvre and Red Pepper Marmalade are also delicious together on bread or crackers. You may wish to serve this on individual plates as a first course. Two slices of chèvre sit on a pool of marmalade.

WHOLE ROASTED GARLIC

3 whole heads garlic

6 tablespoons olive oil

Salt and pepper

1. Preheat oven to 325 degrees.

2. Slice around the garlic ½" up from the base. Peel off the outer skin covering, leaving cloves intact in head.

3. Place garlic in a baking dish.

4. Sprinkle 2 tablespoons olive oil per head. Season with salt and pepper.

5. Bake, basting after 30 minutes.

6. Cover and continue baking for 1 hour more. Serve while still warm.

BAKED CHÈVRE

10- or 11-ounce log chevre

1 egg, beaten

¾ – 1 cup fresh bread crumbs mixed with 1 tablespoon chopped parsley

1. Preheat oven to 450 degrees.

2. Cut cheese in 1" rounds.

3. Dip cheese in beaten egg and then the bread crumbs.

4. Bake on baking tray for 5 minutes until golden.

RED PEPPER MARMALADE

3 red bell peppers

2 large garlic cloves, minced

2 tablespoons olive oil

1. To peel peppers, char in broiler 2" from heat for 20 minutes. Put in a paper bag and steam until cool enough to handle. Peel starting at blossom end. Core and discard seeds.

2. Process all in a food processor until coarsely pureed.

3. Arrange a platter with the sliced chèvre down the center, on top of the pepper puree. Surround with toasted French bread and cloves of roasted garlic.

AUBERGINE SPREAD

My first garden at Uphill Farm was my favorite and quite a challenge. Persistent woodchucks were particularly drawn to my tender eggplants. I persevered, replanted, and used booby traps among other remedies. But in spite of my efforts, they kept reappearing. It was not a stunning victory, but that year I harvested two shiny, purple eggplants! They went into this dish.

A blender or food processor is needed to prepare this. Plan 45 minutes for baking the eggplant, but after that it is quickly prepared. The water in eggplant has a bitter taste, and recipes often call for salting and draining for this reason. In this recipe, after the eggplant bakes, the bitterness can be squeezed out.

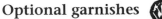

1 medium-sized eggplant, 1 – 1¼ pounds

1–2 cloves garlic

Juice of ½ lemon

Dash of Tabasco

¼ cup olive oil

Salt and pepper to taste

2–3 tablespoons fresh parsley, chopped

2 small whole wheat pitas, cut in quarters

Optional garnishes

1. Preheat oven to 400 degrees.

2. Prick holes in eggplant with a fork and bake on a baking sheet for 45 minutes, until tender.

3. When cool, cut off stem end. Squeeze the eggplant to drain juices out of top. Split, and remove seed bundles and any remaining peel.

4. Add eggplant, garlic, lemon juice, and Tabasco to a blender or food processor. Process until smooth.

5. With the motor still running, add the olive oil in a slow stream.

6. Transfer to a serving bowl. Add salt, pepper, and parsley. Mix through.

7. Cut pitas into triangles. Cover eggplant with additional chopped parsley and set pitas point side up around the dish. Garnish as desired with chopped red onion, chopped parsley, chopped dill, finely chopped egg, black olives, cherry tomatoes, or yogurt.

PREPARATION TIME: 10 minutes
BAKING TIME: 45 minutes

WHOLE WHEAT BLUEBERRY MUFFINS

A basket of moist blueberry muffins is always welcome. I grew little woodland strawberries, juicy raspberries, and blueberries at Uphill Farm. They are so easy to freeze — just freeze unwashed berries on cookie sheets, then seal them in a bag. These wholesome muffins can satisfy hearty appetites any time of day.

1/4 cup butter or margarine

1/2 cup granulated sugar

1 egg, beaten

3/4 cup milk

1/4 teaspoon vanilla extract

1/2 cup whole wheat flour

1/4 cup bran

1 cup unbleached white flour

2 1/2 teaspoons baking powder

1/2 teaspoon salt

1 cup blueberries

1. Heat oven to 425 degrees.

2. Cream butter and sugar. Add beaten egg and stir to combine.

3. Add milk and vanilla. Stir.

4. Combine flours and bran in a separate bowl. Reserve 1 tablespoon of flour-bran mixture.

5. Add remaining dry ingredients and stir.

6. Combine dry mixture with creamed butter. Stir to moisten but do not overmix. (I use a rubber spatula and fold in dry ingredients.)

7. Coat berries with reserved 1 tablespoon flour-bran mixture.

8. Fold berries into batter.

9. Bake in 12 greased muffin tins for 20 minutes.

YIELD: 12 muffins

PREPARATION TIME: 15 minutes

BAKING TIME: 20 minutes

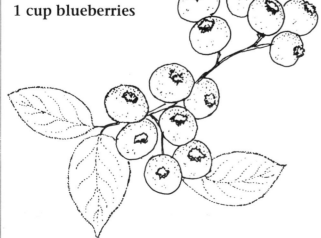

SARAH'S PUMPKIN BREAD

Sarah lived at Uphill in the summer and during her school breaks. This rich pumpkin bread has always been her yearly contribution to Thanksgiving. It's everyone's favorite!

Pumpkin bread is also good when spread with cream cheese the next morning. Be sure to put some bread aside for Pumpkin Bread Pudding (see page 143).

2/3 cup butter or margarine

2 2/3 cups granulated sugar

4 eggs

1 pound prepared pumpkin

2/3 cup water

3 1/3 cups flour

1/2 teaspoon baking soda

1 1/2 teaspoons salt

1 teaspoon cinnamon

1 teaspoon ground cloves

2/3 cup chopped walnuts, optional

2/3 cup chopped dates

1. Preheat oven to 350 degrees.

2. Cream butter and sugar, until fluffy.

3. Beat in 4 eggs, pumpkin, and water.

4. Sift together dry ingredients and stir into pumpkin mixture.

5. Fold in nuts and dates.

6. Spoon batter into 2 loaf pans. Bake for 1 hour.

YIELD: 2 loaves
PREPARATION TIME: 25 minutes
BAKING TIME: 1 hour

CATHARINE'S OATMEAL & MOLASSES BREAD

Inscribed inside my engagement ring is: 19 November 1893 CLF from APR. The ring belonged to my husband's great grandmother, Catharine Lucy Farr Robinson, and this is her bread recipe. It is a favorite of ours.

Besides its wonderful texture and flavor, this bread has an extra bonus: start it the night before (there is no kneading) and it rises overnight. In the morning, stir it down and pop it in the oven. The rest of the household will awaken to the yeasty aroma and taste of warm bread. Save one loaf to have with supper. A very easy, very delicious recipe.

1 cup oatmeal

2 cups boiling water

1 yeast cake

3 tablespoons warm water

1/2 cup black molasses

1 tablespoon salt

4 cups unbleached white flour

Make this sponge the night before.

1. Soak the oatmeal for 30 minutes in the boiling water.

2. Dissolve yeast in the warm water. Add to oatmeal.

3. Stir in molasses and salt.

4. Slowly sift in flour.

5. Mix well with a wooden spoon.

6. Put in a bowl to rise overnight. Cover with a clean tea towel.

In the morning:

1. Preheat oven to 350 degrees.

2. Stir dough down and divide into two, buttered 4" x 8" loaf pans.

3. Let rise for about 1 hour.

4. Bake for 1 hour.

YIELD: 2 loaves

PREPARATION TIME: Less than 30 minutes plus rising times

BAKING TIME: 1 hour

VARIATION: Substitute 1 cup whole wheat flour for 1 of the 4 cups of white flour.

SWEET CREAM SCONES

When winter came, we'd settle indoors by the wood stove. Afternoons lingered, letters got written, and crossword puzzles were done. It was the perfect time of year for tea and scones, always with strawberry-rhubarb jam made the summer before.

1²/3 cups flour

1/3 cup whole wheat flour (2 cups white flour, total, may be used instead of 1/3 cup whole wheat flour)

1 tablespoon baking powder

2 tablespoons granulated sugar

1/2 teaspoon salt

1/4 cup butter, preferably sweet butter

2 eggs

1/3 cup light cream

2 teaspoons granulated sugar

1. Preheat oven to 400 degrees.

2. Combine flours, baking powder, 2 tablespoons sugar, and salt.

3. Cut in the butter with 2 knives until the mixture is well combined and resembles coarse meal.

4. Before beating the eggs, remove 2 tablespoons of the whites. Reserve.

5. Beat the eggs, and add along with the cream to the butter mixture.

6. Knead on a lightly floured board, just until the dough sticks together.

7. Divide dough in half.

8. Gently roll or pat each half into a circle 6" in diameter, and 1" thick.

9. Cut the circles into quarters. You will have 8 triangles.

10. Brush the tops with the reserved egg whites and sprinkle with remaining 2 teaspoons sugar.

11. Place on greased cookie sheets and bake for 15 minutes. Serve immediately with sweet butter and preserves.

YIELD: 8 scones
PREPARATION TIME: 15 minutes
BAKING TIME: 15 minutes

SEASONAL SALADS

Broccoli & Pasta Salad with Sun-dried Tomato Vinaigrette

Marinated Asparagus

Chicken & Orzo Salad

Hungarian Rice Salad

Shrimp & Potato Salad

Chicken & Greens with Orange Vinaigrette

Green Bean & New Potato Salad

Braised Leeks in Crème Fraîche

Red Cabbage & Blue Cheese Salad

Lentil & Brown Rice Salad

Marinated Chick Pea Salad

Salad Dressings:

Favorite Vinaigrette

In-the-Bowl Dressing

Lemon-Dijon Dressing

Honey-Soy Vinaigrette

Sour Cream Dressing

Warm Bacon Dressing

Broccoli & Pasta Salad with Sun-dried Tomato Vinaigrette

We've always planted and harvested broccoli early, before caterpillars appear. This is one of our first "garden meals." Toss it in a big bowl and carry to the pond, the stone wall, or orchard. The flavors improve with time.

3 sun-dried tomato halves

1 clove garlic, minced

1 shallot, finely chopped

1/4 teaspoon salt

3 tablespoons red wine vinegar

1/3 cup olive oil

1/2 pound dried, small pasta: tortellini, bow ties, or shells

1 cup broccoli, cut into florets

1. Simmer tomato halves in enough water to cover for 3 minutes. Drain and mince.

2. In a bowl, mix minced tomatoes, garlic, shallot, and salt with vinegar.

3. Whisk in olive oil until emulsified.

4. Cook pasta and drain.

5. While warm, toss with vinaigrette.

6. Barely cook broccoli, 1–2 minutes. Toss with pasta.

7. Serve at room temperature.

YIELD: 4–5 servings

PREPARATION TIME: 20 minutes

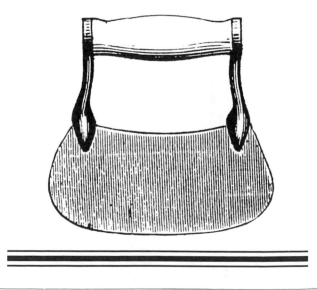

MARINATED ASPARAGUS

There was an old and very productive asparagus bed at Uphill Farm. In spring, we made asparagus soups, souffles, and omelets. This easy-to-prepare salad is one of my favorites.

1 pound asparagus

Pinch salt

1 shallot, finely chopped

1 tablespoon red wine vinegar, or balsamic vinegar

1 teaspoon lemon juice

1/2 teaspoon Dijon-style mustard

Salt and pepper

3 tablespoons olive oil

1. Bring 2" of water to a boil in a skillet large enough to lay asparagus flat. Add a pinch of salt.

2. Wash asparagus in cold water. Break off the tough base of each. Remove scales if they are large or sandy.

3. Place spears in the boiling water. Quickly return water to a boil, then uncover and gently simmer.

4. Cook for 5–7 minutes. Do not over-cook. Asparagus should be slightly crisp.

5. Drain. Place in an oval dish to marinate.

6. Place the shallot in a small bowl. Stir in the vinegar, lemon juice, mustard, salt, and pepper. Whisk in olive oil.

7. Pour marinade over warm asparagus. Allow to marinate at room temperature until cool; then refrigerate until serving. Return to room temperature before serving.

8. Serve on individual salad plates, spooning vinaigrette and shallots over each serving, or lay spears on a white oval platter and top with marinade.

YIELD: 4 first course servings or 2 servings for real asparagus fans

PREPARATION TIME: 10 minutes

COOKING TIME: 5 minutes

CHICKEN & ORZO SALAD

On those first warm evenings in spring, when the light lasts and the peepers racket, we'd walk up the hill and have supper by the pond. This was the dinner we'd bring along. It's easily packed and delicious with olives, French bread, and herb butter. Bring a bottle of wine to toast the coming season!

$3/4$ cup blanched, sliced almonds

2 whole chicken breasts

$1^1/2$ – 2 cups chicken broth

2 cups orzo (after cooking)

6 tablespoons olive oil

2 tablespoons red wine vinegar

2 tablespoons lemon juice

Dash Tabasco

3 tablespoons combination of chives and parsley

Salt and pepper

1 tablespoon red onion, minced

1 tablespoon chopped parsley

Spinach leaves and navel orange sections, optional

1. Toast almonds in a 425 degree oven for 5 minutes. Let cool.

2. In a covered pot, simmer chicken breast in broth to cover for 15 minutes. Let cool in liquid.

3. When cool, cut into bite-sized pieces.

4. Cook orzo according to package directions. Drain.

5. While pasta is still warm, toss with oil, vinegar, lemon juice, Tabasco, parsley, chives, salt, and pepper.

6. Add chicken, red onion, and almonds. Toss well and spoon onto a platter. Surround with spinach and orange sections tossed in a vinaigrette flavored with orange peel.

7. Sprinkle remaining parsley on top.

8. Refrigerate until serving or serve at room temperature.

YIELD: 4 servings

PREPARATION TIME: 30 minutes

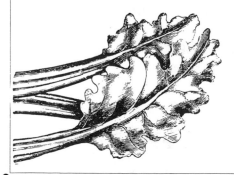

HUNGARIAN RICE SALAD

There is probably little that is Hungarian about this salad except it is colorful and reminds me of my grandmother who was from Hungary. "It's the gypsy in you," she used to tell me, when as a child I insisted on wearing bright colors, especially red. This rice dish complements a variety of summer meals. Use only garden-fresh tomatoes. Make the dressing in advance and refrigerate it. Combine the rice, tomatoes, and onions ahead, but toss with the dressing just prior to serving.

2 – 2¹/₂ cups cooked rice

4–5 tomatoes, coarsely cut into bite-sized pieces

1 onion, finely chopped

Salt and pepper

¹/₄ cup olive oil

¹/₄ cup red wine vinegar

1–2 tablespoons granulated sugar

4 tablespoons chopped parsley and/or snipped chives

Pinch salt and pepper

1. Combine rice, tomatoes, and onion. Add salt and pepper to taste.

2. Mix olive oil, vinegar, sugar, salt, and pepper together in a small jar.

3. Pour over rice salad, and mix well.

4. Sprinkle parsley or chives over all.

YIELD: 5–6 servings
PREPARATION TIME: Under 15 minutes

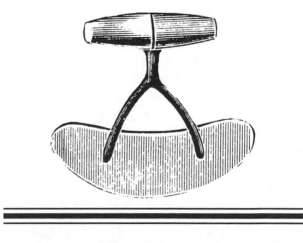

SHRIMP & POTATO SALAD

Most years we grew potatoes, shallots, and tarragon in the garden — all Owen's favorites. One year I made this salad for his birthday picnic — combining favorite vegetables with seafood.

Prepare the salad in advance; it needs to marinate at least 4 hours. For serving, spoon the salad in the center of a platter, and surround with blanched, whole marinated green beans sprinkled with shallots.

1½ **pounds medium-sized shrimp, cooked and peeled**

8 **small red potatoes**

3 **shallots, finely chopped**

Salt and pepper

3 **tablespoons fresh tarragon, chopped, or** 2½ **teaspoons dried**

1 **cup dry vermouth or white wine**

2 **tablespoons Cognac or brandy**

3 **tablespoons lemon juice**

Dash Tabasco

½ **cup olive oil**

1. Wash potatoes, but do not peel. Boil until just tender, not mushy. Slice into ¼" slices.

2. While still warm, put a generous layer of potatoes in a large bowl. Sprinkle the layer with some of the shallots, salt, pepper, tarragon, and then some vermouth.

3. Cover this with a layering of shrimp. The shrimp will make a sparser layer than the potatoes. Repeat, sprinkling with shallots, etc.

4. Continue layering and sprinkling until the shrimp and potatoes are used.

5. Cover and refrigerate for 4 hours, or overnight.

6. Just prior to serving, combine Cognac, lemon juice, salt, pepper, Tabasco, and olive oil.

7. Pour over salad and toss.

YIELD: 6 servings

PREPARATION TIME: 30 minutes

VARIATION: Ham may be substituted for the shrimp.

Chicken & Greens with Orange Vinaigrette

This is a year-round main dish salad. Use a variety of greens, according to your personal taste; the orange vinaigrette brings it all together. It is a favorite salad of mine — light, but rich in taste.

SALAD

2 whole chicken breasts, split

Salt and pepper

1 tablespoon olive oil

3 tablespoons orange juice

1 ounce sliced almonds

4–6 cups mixed greens

2 tablespoons shallot or red onion, finely chopped

Roquefort or blue cheese, crumbled to taste

DRESSING

3 tablespoons orange juice

2 tablespoons wine vinegar

6 tablespoons olive oil

1 clove garlic, minced

Pinch salt

Pinch grated orange rind

1. Salt and pepper chicken breasts.

2. Saute chicken in olive oil until white on each side.

3. Pour orange juice in skillet, raise heat, and continue to brown on both sides as juice cooks away, about 10–15 minutes total.

4. Cool chicken and slice into bite-sized pieces.

5. Brown almonds on tray in oven, shaking tray as they color.

6. Tear greens into bite-sized pieces. Toss with shallot.

7. Whisk together dressing ingredients. Toss over greens.

8. Layer chicken on top of greens. Sprinkle with almonds and Roquefort or blue cheese.

YIELD: 4 servings

PREPARATION TIME: 30 minutes

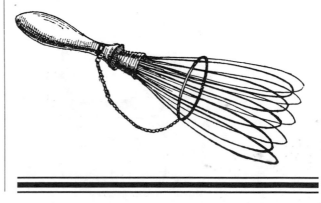

Green Bean & New Potato Salad

If you're lucky enough to grow your own potatoes, harvest some when they are only pecan-sized. They can be sauteed whole or halved in olive oil and salt — it takes only a few minutes. Added beans give a nice crunch! This salad is best when made ahead of time, allowing the flavors to meld. If it is made early in the day, it may be refrigerated, but allow sufficient time to return to room temperature before serving.

3 tablespoons red wine vinegar

5–6 tablespoons olive oil

1 clove garlic, minced

1/2 teaspoon salt

Freshly ground black pepper

6 new or small red potatoes

3/4 pound small green beans

2 tablespoons chopped red onion, or shallots

4 tablespoons fresh parsley, chopped

1. Combine vinegar, oil, garlic, salt, and pepper in a medium-sized serving bowl.

2. Wash potatoes; do not peel. Cook until just tender; the time will vary according to the size of your potatoes. Do not overcook.

3. Drain and cool potatoes, until they can be handled. They can be slipped out of their skins, or leave the skins on. Cut in 1/8" slices.

4. Toss the warm potatoes in the vinaigrette.

5. Wash the beans and break off the tips. Steam briefly until just crisp tender. Rinse under cold water. Pat dry.

6. Toss the beans with the potatoes.

7. Sprinkle parsley and red onion over all.

YIELD: 4–6 servings

PREPARATION TIME: 30 minutes plus cooling

FRESH FROM THE GARDEN — HERBS

Growing your own herbs to use in salads and cooking is easy and rewarding. Nothing compares to the taste of fresh basil, tarragon, dill, or oregano. And, best of all, you don't need to have a garden to grow them. Herbs do fine in flowerpots on windowsills, patios, and fire escapes. Pick all summer from the bottom leaves. When harvesting in the fall, cut only the top third of the plant, tie in small bunches, and hang in a cool, dark place. Quick drying herbs preserves their flavor and color. Here are some tips and ideas that will put fresh herbs to good use in your cooking.

❦ When recipes call for herbs, choose to use fresh ones if possible. One teaspoon of a dried herb is equal to a tablespoon of fresh.

❦ Herbs can flavor vinegar. Tarragon dries well and also makes delicious vinegar; place sprigs in cider or white wine vinegar. Make some in empty, small wine bottles and give as gifts.

❦ Fresh herbs add to the taste of salad dressings in a delightful way. Add chopped basil, chives, chervil, oregano, savory, or tarragon to the greens, then toss with a vinaigrette. Experiment with other herbs. Classic vinaigrette proportions are 3 parts oil to 1 part vinegar. This can be varied to taste. Use 1/2 vegetable, peanut, or walnut oil for a lighter dressing. Add herbs, garlic, mustard, lemon juice, and always lots of freshly ground pepper.

❦ Olive oil is a wonderful base for flavored oils. Try adding crushed garlic with a single herb: rosemary, basil, thyme, sage, or oregano. Make only enough for immediate use.

❦ Garden herb cheese is delicious on crackers, crusty bread, carrots, celery, and other crunchy vegetables. Simply drain small curd cottage cheese and mix well with cream cheese. Stir in finely minced garlic, shallots, and a combination of herbs. Chives, dill, and sage make wonderful additions to soft cheese. Wrap in cheese cloth and press into a covered bowl. Refrigerate for 24 hours.

❦ Enjoy delicious pesto made with fresh basil. Combine 2 cups fresh basil leaves, 3 cloves garlic, 1/2 teaspoon salt and pepper in processor. Chop leaves and add 1/4 cup olive oil in a slow stream. This simple homemade sauce for pasta is so much better than most store-bought pesto — and is less expensive, too! Spread pesto on French bread and add cheese, tomatoes, and lettuce for a flavorful sandwich.

❦ Rosemary adds a great flavor to many dishes, including chicken, fish, salads, and potatoes. Toss walnut-sized red potatoes with olive oil, salt, garlic, and plenty of rosemary. Cook, shaking pan occasionally, until potatoes are done.

BRAISED LEEKS IN CRÈME FRAÎCHE

*At Uphill, I came to depend on leeks as a delicious and subtle flavoring for soups and stews. They are also incredibly versatile; try creamed leeks on toast, in omelets, with cream cheese and ham for a wonderful main course soup. Braised leeks, allowed to cool in flavorful sauces, make a lovely first course, such as the following braised leeks in **crème fraîche**. Both the leeks and sauce can be prepared ahead of time and combined just prior to serving.*

8 leeks, trimmed of all but 1" of the green and well rinsed

2 tablespoons butter or margarine

$1/2$ teaspoon salt

1 cup crème fraîche or sour cream

$1/2$ teaspoon curry

1 small clove garlic, finely minced

1 teaspoon grated horseradish

2 tablespoons cider vinegar

Chives and chive blossoms, optional garnish

1. Combine leeks, butter, and salt in a covered casserole. Add water to cover.

2. Bring to a boil, lower heat, and simmer until barely tender. Test with a fork. Cooking time will vary according to size of the leeks, but avoid overcooking.

3. Drain leeks well. Refrigerate until serving.

4. In a small bowl, combine remaining ingredients and stir well.

5. Arrange leeks on a serving platter or individual salad plates. Spoon crème fraîche over them.

6. Garnish with snipped chives and chive blossoms.

YIELD: 4 servings
PREPARATION TIME: 15 minutes
COOKING TIME: 10 minutes

CRÈME FRAÎCHE

Crème fraîche is a distinctively tart soured cream, widely used in French cooking. It can be used as a base for salad dressings, sauce for vegetables and soups, and dolloped on fruits and berries, either sweetened or plain.

*You can now buy a commercial **crème fraîche** at some markets, but it is easy to prepare at home and will keep about two weeks, refrigerated.*

2 cups heavy cream

2 tablespoons buttermilk

1. Combine liquids.

2. Pour into a large jar with cover. Leave out at room temperature, away from drafts, overnight. The cream will thicken and have a slightly acidic taste.

3. Store in the refrigerator.

RED CABBAGE & BLUE CHEESE SALAD

When the growing season for lettuce ends, so does my taste for green salad. Cabbage is one vegetable my family and I have always enjoyed during the colder months. This recipe blends two strong ingredients — blue cheese and mustard — to create a salad that's sure to make your mouth water.

1 head red cabbage

3/4 cup blue cheese, crumbled

3/4 cup fresh parsley, chopped

1/4 cup Dijon-style mustard

1 1/2 cups mayonnaise

1. Remove outer cabbage leaves and core.

2. Shred the cabbage and put in a mixing bowl.

3. Add half the cheese and parsley; toss.

4. Mix mustard and mayonnaise. Stir into cabbage and toss well.

5. Top with remaining cheese and parsley.

6. Refrigerate for two or more hours.

YIELD: 8 servings
PREPARATION TIME: 10 minutes
REFRIGERATION TIME: 2 hours

LENTIL & BROWN RICE SALAD

This zesty winter salad is the perfect way to enliven the simplest of suppers. Its tangy vinaigrette flavors the lentils and brown rice to create a perfect side dish for almost any meal. Garnish with fresh parsley or apple slices.

3 3/4 cups water

Salt

1 cup brown rice

1 cup lentils

4 scallions, thinly sliced

1/2 red onion, finely chopped

2 red or green peppers, finely chopped

3 tablespoons fresh parsley, chopped

3 tablespoons chopped raisins

3 tablespoons chopped nuts

VINAIGRETTE

1/2 teaspoon dry mustard

1/2 teaspoon granulated sugar, optional

6 tablespoons red wine vinegar

Salt and pepper

3/4 cup olive oil or olive/vegetable oil mixture

1. Bring 4 cups water to a boil. Add salt.

2. Rinse rice and lentils together in cold water.

3. Add to boiling water. Cover and reduce to a simmer. Cook 35 minutes.

4. While they are cooking, prepare a vinaigrette by combining mustard, sugar, vinegar, salt, and pepper. Whisk in olive oil.

5. Transfer cooked rice and lentils to a large mixing bowl. While still warm, toss in vinaigrette. Let cool.

6. Add remaining ingredients and toss.

YIELD: 6–8 servings

PREPARATION TIME: under 1 hour

VARIATIONS: Toss in other fresh vegetables, apples, or whatever appeals.

Marinated Chick Pea Salad

I first made this salad in winter. There were no fresh greens or vegetables in Uphill's cool larder. We all liked it so much, that it became a year-round staple. It goes well with marinated lamb, or grilled fish.

1 (16-ounce) can chick peas, drained

1 clove garlic, minced

1/2 small red onion, finely chopped (or substitute a shallot)

2–4 tablespoons fresh parsley, chopped

3 tablespoons red wine vinegar or lemon juice (or combination of both)

3 tablespoons olive oil

Salt and pepper

1. Drain chick peas.

2. In a separate bowl, combine remaining ingredients and whisk until well blended.

3. Add chick peas and toss.

4. Let marinate for 30 minutes or more.

YIELD: 6 servings
PREPARATION TIME: 5 minutes
MARINATE: 30 minutes minimum

HUILE d'OLIVE
vierge
IMPORTED®

SALAD DRESSINGS

Salads are a matter of personal taste, and creativity. In summer, with its almost endless options, salads can be as diverse and imaginative as your spirit. In winter, we have to dig further, raiding the larder in lieu of the garden to give salads balance — both nutritional and culinary.

The key to salad making is in a light touch: dressings that enhance, rather than mask; vegetables simply prepared, revealing their individual textures and flavors, never served icy cold; stereotypes avoided by serving the salad when most appropriate — before, during, and after the main course (if not as the main course).

My favorite salad? Boston lettuce tossed with a simple shallot vinaigrette.

FAVORITE VINAIGRETTE

Most recipes suggest a vinegar to oil ratio of 1:3. However, I enjoy sharper dressings, with a ratio of 3:5. Test to find your preference.

1 shallot, finely chopped

¼ teaspoon salt

3 tablespoons red wine vinegar

5 tablespoons olive oil (or part olive oil, part vegetable oil)

Freshly ground pepper

1. Pour vinegar over shallots. Season with salt and pepper.

2. Stir or shake in covered jar.

3. Whisk in oil.

IN-THE-BOWL DRESSING

1. Rub garlic clove over salad bowl.

2. Add washed, dry greens.

3. Spoon olive oil over leaves and mix.

4. Add a little vinegar. Toss to coat greens. Sprinkle with salt and pepper. Mix well.

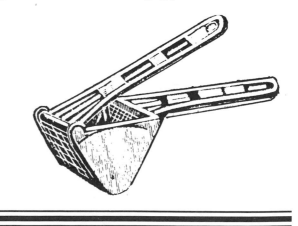

LEMON-DIJON DRESSING

Juice of 1/2 lemon
(approximately 2 tablespoons)

1/2 teaspoon Dijon-style mustard

1/3 cup oil

Freshly ground black pepper

1. Whisk together lemon juice and mustard.

2. Continue whisking while adding oil in a slow stream.

3. Season with pepper.

HONEY-SOY VINAIGRETTE

This is a light vinaigrette that is especially good tossed with any combination of blanched winter vegetables — carrots, broccoli, peppers, water chestnuts, celery. Add leftover rice, and turn this into a main dish winter salad.

1/3 cup water

1/3 cup peanut or corn oil

1/3 cup cider vinegar

2 tablespoons light soy sauce

2 tablespoons minced scallions

2 teaspoons honey

1/4 teaspoon ground ginger

1. Combine ingredients in a small jar with a tight-fitting lid.

2. Shake well to mix.

SOUR CREAM DRESSING

1/2 cup sour cream or yogurt
(half of this can be mayonnaise)

2 tablespoons vinegar

2 teaspoons granulated sugar

1 clove garlic, minced

1/2 teaspoon salt

1/2 teaspoon dry mustard

1/4 cup milk

1. Combine all ingredients.

2. Refrigerate 4 hours or overnight.

WARM BACON DRESSING

A warm country dressing, excellent for a winter salad of spinach and flavored croutons.

4 slices bacon, cut in 1" pieces

2 teaspoons brown sugar

2 tablespoons cider vinegar

Freshly ground black pepper

1. Fry bacon. Do not drain.

2. Add brown sugar. Stir; then add vinegar. Continue cooking for 1 minute.

3. Season with pepper to taste.

4. Toss bacon and dressing over greens. Serve immediately.

GLORIOUS VEGETABLES

Spicy Stewed Eggplant

Brigitte's Onion Tart

Fried Green Tomatoes

On-the-Grill Vegetables

Buttery Baked Corn

Green Beans, Potatoes, & Cornmeal Dumplings

Lacy Leek & Potato Cakes

Artichoke Risotto

Sauerkraut & Apples

A Galaxy of Onions

Golden Potato Puree

Wintry Potato Casserole

Ginger & Garlic Winter Squash

Spicy Stewed Eggplant

This is a versatile dish, served hot over rice or with Vermont Corn Bread (see page 102). The leftovers are great at room temperature for a picnic or weekend lunch.

1 large eggplant

1 teaspoon salt

1/4 cup olive oil

1 large or 2 medium onions, coarsely chopped

4 cloves garlic, minced

8–12 ounces mushrooms, coarsely chopped

1 large red pepper, chopped

1/2 – 1 teaspoon crushed red pepper

Salt and pepper

1 large can tomatoes, drained

1 1/2 teaspoons fresh basil, or 1/2 teaspoon dried

1. Chop eggplant in 3/8" pieces. Sprinkle with salt and allow to drain 30 minutes.

2. Heat oil in large skillet. Saute onion and garlic until softened.

3. Add mushrooms, continuing to saute until mushrooms give off liquid that then cooks away.

4. Dry eggplant between paper towels.

5. Add eggplant and pepper to skillet.

6. Sprinkle with red pepper, salt, and pepper.

7. Cook, stirring occasionally for 15 minutes.

8. Add drained tomatoes and basil. Break up tomatoes with wooden spoon and cook for additional 15 minutes.

YIELD: 3–4 servings

PREPARATION TIME: 40 minutes

COOKING TIME: 30 minutes

BRIGITTE'S ONION TART

Brigitte is a wonderful and generous cook. This is the tart remembered from her childhood days in an Alsatian village in France. It is a delicious first course, or, when served with a salad, it can be the main course for a light supper.

6 tablespoons butter or margarine

3–4 large onions, coarsely chopped

Salt and pepper

2 slices Canadian bacon, optional

1 tablespoon flour

1/2 cup milk

1 egg

1 cup imported Swiss cheese, grated

1 pie shell, unbaked
(see page 114)

1. Preheat oven to 400 degrees.

2. In a large skillet, saute onions in 4 tablespoons melted butter for a few minutes. Do not brown.

3. Season with salt and pepper. Cover pan, lower heat, and let onions soften for 20 minutes.

4. Add bacon and stir.

5. Add flour and stir over low heat for 2 minutes.

6. Whisk in milk and egg until thickened. Season with salt and pepper.

7. Put grated cheese in bottom of the pie shell.

8. Pour egg mixture over cheese. Dot with remaining butter.

9. Bake 30 minutes.

YIELD: 8 servings
PREPARATION TIME: 20 minutes
COOKING TIME: 30 minutes

FRIED GREEN TOMATOES

If your garden is anything like mine, at the end of the season you'll have plenty of green tomatoes on hand. I like them so much that I'll pick unripe tomatoes in early August just to enjoy this dish.

4 green tomatoes

Salt

$3/4$ cup cornmeal

2 tablespoons olive oil

2 tablespoons butter or margarine

$1/3$ cup brown sugar, optional

$1/3$ cup half-and-half, optional

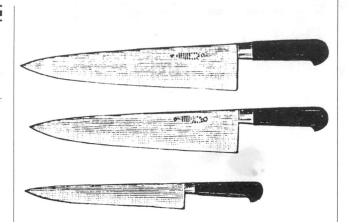

1. Slice tomatoes $1/3$" thick. Sprinkle with salt and coat with cornmeal.

2. Heat oil and butter over medium-high heat. Add tomato slices in a single layer.

3. Sprinkle bits of brown sugar on tops. Turn when golden on bottom.

4. Sprinkle sugar on top and continue cooking until soft.

5. Turn again to melt sugar.

6. Remove and serve on a warm platter.

7. Pour cream in skillet and stir up brown bits. Spoon over tomatoes if desired.

YIELD: 4 servings

COOKING TIME: 15 minutes

FRESH FROM THE GARDEN — TOMATOES

Grow tomatoes! Even if you don't garden, grow tomatoes. As with herbs, you may grow them in pots almost anywhere — even on a city roof or fire escape.

In Vermont we are limited to when we can enjoy fresh tomatoes but not to how much we can eat . . . .

❧ I think tomatoes are best when simply sliced and sprinkled with salt, pepper, and fresh basil. Drizzle with a good olive oil and vinegar. Vary by adding chopped red onions, shallots, or parsley.

❧ Toss coarsely chopped tomatoes, cucumbers, and red onions with vinaigrette for a quick salad that is rich in garden-fresh flavor.

❧ For the best-ever tomato sandwiches, slice tomatoes on French bread, and top with olive oil, salt, pepper, and basil. Only after many of these sandwiches, do we waiver and add cheese, sometimes melted over the top.

❧ Thickly slice green tomatoes, dip in cornmeal, and saute in butter. Brown sugar and cream can be added to the pan drippings, after tomatoes are cooked tender. See page 48 for Fried Green Tomatoes.

❧ To make fresh tomato soup, simply simmer carrots, onions, and green or red peppers until soft. Briefly cook tomatoes and puree all through a food mill.

❧ Cherry tomatoes, just picked and still warm from the sun, are delicious. Try filling halves with pesto or herb cheese for hors d'oeuvres. Or, saute them in butter, olive oil, salt, pepper, and basil.

❧ Marinate sliced tomatoes in olive oil, balsamic vinegar, salt, pepper, and basil or oregano. Spread on oven-toasted French bread for bruschetta.

❧ Toss marinated, chopped tomatoes with cubed Italian or French bread. Add chopped onion and cucumbers for Panzanella, an Italian salad.

ON-THE-GRILL VEGETABLES

Beyond the back porch at Uphill, we had an outdoor cooking pit — a hand-dug hole that we built a fire in. As the wood burned down, food was cooked on an oven shelf that covered the pit.

Grilling highlights the natural sweetness of vegetables. Eat them right off the grill with crusty bread to sop up vegetable juices, or tossed with pasta and a little olive oil.

A combination of the following ripe, fresh vegetables:

> **eggplant**
>
> **summer squash**
>
> **tomatoes**
>
> **leeks**
>
> **sweet peppers**
>
> **mushrooms**
>
> **garlic cloves, unpeeled**

1. Light grill. Wait for coals to turn gray.

2. Prepare vegetables by slicing eggplant and squash in 1/2" rounds. Cut tomatoes in half. Discard green tops of leeks, leaving roots intact. Halve lengthwise and wash well to remove any sand. Slice peppers in 3" pieces. Leave mushrooms and garlic cloves whole.

3. Grill vegetables 4"– 6" from coals, on a fine wire mesh if available.

4. Cook slowly, turning periodically. The leeks should be slightly charred and tender.

5. Let vegetables cool slightly in a large bowl. Sprinkle with basil.

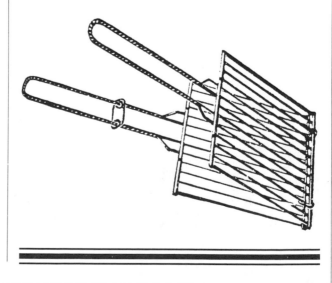

BUTTERY BAKED CORN

Freshly picked golden corn, cooked immediately, is a treasure, as any home gardener knows — especially in Vermont, where the season is so short and raccoons are so determined! This preparation is a slight variation from the daily "on the cob" eating usually done in August.

1. Preheat oven to 350 degrees.

2. Mix kernels with the half stick butter. Season with salt and pepper.

3. Put corn in a small souffle or oven dish.

4. Bake 30 minutes until top is golden.

YIELD: 4–5 servings

PREPARATION TIME: 5 minutes

COOKING TIME: 30 minutes

VARIATION: Try this with frozen corn. It's quite good, and a reminder of sweet summer eating!

4 cups corn, freshly sliced from the cob

4 tablespoons butter or margarine, melted

Salt and pepper

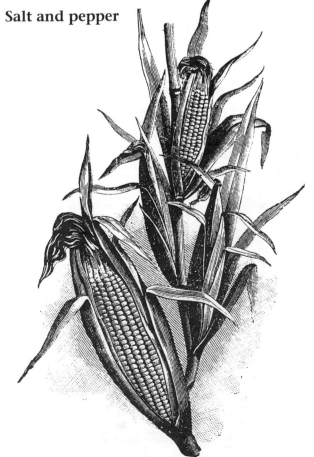

Green Beans, Potatoes, & Cornmeal Dumplings

When I was overwhelmed with green beans and couldn't even keep up with freezing them, I'd prepare this dish — it's a great use for those big beans that were left on the vine too long. A frugal farm dish that tastes good wherever and however you live.

2 pounds green beans

1/4-pound chunk salt pork or bacon

1/2 teaspoon salt

4 medium potatoes

DUMPLINGS

1 cup flour

1 teaspoon salt

2 teaspoons baking powder

1 cup cornmeal

1 egg, beaten

3/4 cup milk

1. Place beans, salt pork, and salt in a large pot. Add water to almost cover.

2. Cover pot and bring to a boil. Uncover and slowly simmer for 20 minutes.

3. Wash, halve, and if desired, peel the potatoes. Add to simmering liquid and cook 30 minutes more.

4. While simmering, prepare dumplings. Combine dry ingredients. In a separate bowl, mix the egg and milk together. Combine egg mixture with dry ingredients. Do not overmix.

5. Drop by rounded teaspoonfuls on top of the boiling greens and potatoes. Cover pot and cook for 15 minutes.

6. Serve beans, potatoes, and dumplings with chopped bacon, or salt pork and pot juices.

YIELD: 4 servings

PREPARATION TIME: 15 minutes

COOKING TIME: 65 minutes

FRESH FROM THE GARDEN — GARLIC

I can't imagine cooking without garlic. And growing garlic is such a pleasure. Buy one large head and put in the freezer for a week to allow it to go dormant. Separate cloves and plant them in the garden or in a deep pot. In Vermont, we plant garlic in the fall.

❦ Crushed garlic cloves can be used to flavor virgin olive oil. This makes a delicious alternative to butter with crusty bread. Place it on the table in a small saucer, and simply dip your bread. Remember to refrigerate leftover garlic oil; it will spoil if left at room temperature for an extended period of time.

❦ For a fiery pasta dish, saute 2 cloves minced garlic and 1 tablespoon red pepper flakes in 1/4 cup olive oil. Toss with hot pasta.

❦ Aioli is a traditional, homemade garlic mayonnaise. In a food processor, puree 8 cloves of garlic. Add two beaten egg yolks, lemon juice, and a bit of Dijon-style mustard. Process. Slowly add 1 1/2 cups olive oil in while processing. Serve with small, new potatoes, green beans, mushrooms, or pea pods.

❦ Mix crushed garlic into prepared mayonnaise. This is good with melted cheese sandwiches or salami on baguettes.

❦ Add one or two garlic cloves to the water while boiling potatoes. Then, mash together for flavorful mashed potatoes.

LACY LEEK & POTATO CAKES

Potatoes always were a staple "on the hill" — we cooked them so many different ways. A heaping platter of these will complement roast chicken or tender pork. They can also be the focus of the meal when served with creamy tomato soup and steamed greens.

2 large eggs, beaten

1/2 cup flour

Salt

1/4 cup beer

3 leeks, white part only, washed well, finely chopped

2 baking potatoes

Canola or other vegetable oil

1. Mix eggs, flour, salt, beer, and leeks.

2. Grate potatoes and squeeze out moisture. Blend into egg mixture.

3. Heat 1/2" oil in large skillet.

4. Form potato mixture into 3" cakes.

5. Fry until golden on each side. Cook in batches.

6. Drain on paper towels and keep warm in a 200 degree oven.

YIELD: 6 servings
PREPARATION TIME: 10 minutes
COOKING TIME: 10 minutes

ARTICHOKE RISOTTO

This creamy rice dish is best made with Italian rice. Carolina rice is close, but converted rice will not do. Cook vegetables in with the rice, and serve it as a main dish.

1 package frozen artichoke hearts, defrosted, or 1 can, drained and quartered

6 tablespoons butter or margarine

1 onion, chopped

1 clove garlic, minced

1 cup rice (Arborio or Carolina-type)

1/2 cup white wine or vermouth

3 1/2–4 cups chicken or vegetable broth

1 tablespoon lemon juice

1. Cut thawed artichokes into 3 pieces each. Set aside to drain.

2. Melt 4 tablespoons butter and gently saute onion and garlic.

3. Stir in rice; continue stirring until grains are transparent, 1–2 minutes.

4. Heat wine, and stir into rice until liquid is absorbed.

5. Stir in artichokes.

6. Heat stock to a gentle simmer. Add 1/2 cup at a time. Stir for about 20 minutes. Rice will be creamy.

7. Just before serving, stir in remaining butter and lemon juice.

YIELD: 4 servings

SAUERKRAUT & APPLES

In fall, baskets of bright red apples filled the farmhouse. They waited to be dried, made into tangy sauces, or individually wrapped for storage. I used them in cooking as much as possible, often filling the kitchen with their sweet aroma. Serve this simple, satisfying autumn dish with boiled potatoes, rye bread, and cold beer or cider.

2 pounds sauerkraut, rinsed (preferably freshly packed, not canned)

1 cup water

1/4 pound bacon

1 onion, coarsely chopped

2 apples, chopped

1/2 teaspoon caraway seeds

1. Simmer sauerkraut in water for 10 minutes.

2. Cook bacon in a large, heavy skillet. As fat renders, add onions and apples. Stir and continue cooking in bacon fat until onion is tender.

3. Drain sauerkraut. Toss with bacon mixture and caraway seeds.

4. Serve hot — perhaps on a pewter plate — surrounded by boiled potatoes.

YIELD: 4–6 servings
PREPARATION TIME: 5 minutes
COOKING TIME: 10 minutes

A GALAXY OF ONIONS

I made this years ago for Thanksgiving. Using five different types of onions, garlic, and parsley from my garden, I created a creamy blend that was a great hit. It's been requested for Thanksgiving ever since.

It can all be prepared in advance, except the final baking — a helpful feature in the frenzy of holiday cooking or a company supper.

3–4 tablespoons butter

1/2 pound shallots, whole or halved if particularly large

6–8 leeks, white part only, split and well rinsed, cut in 1" rounds (not smaller)

1 large yellow onion, halved lengthwise and sliced in large wedges

1 large red onion, halved lengthwise and sliced in large wedges

2 cloves garlic, minced

12 pearl onions

2 cups half-and-half

Salt and pepper

Grated nutmeg

1/4 cup minced parsley

3 tablespoons fresh bread crumbs

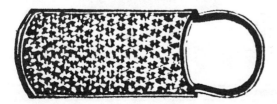

1. Melt butter in large skillet or Dutch oven.

2. Add the garlic and the onion varieties, except the pearl onions.

3. Toss gently over low heat until onions soften, about 20–30 minutes. Do not brown.

4. While onions are cooking, drop pearl onions into boiling water and simmer for 5 minutes. Drain. Make a slit across root ends; onions will slip out of their skins. Add the parboiled pearl onions to the cooked onions.

5. Add the half-and-half to the onions. Bring to a boil and simmer until cream is reduced and thickened, about 10 minutes.

6. Season to taste with salt, pepper, and nutmeg. Stir in the parsley.

7. Preheat oven to 475 degrees.

8. Spoon into a buttered, shallow baking dish. Sprinkle with bread crumbs.

9. Bake 15 minutes until golden.

YIELD: 8–10 servings
PREPARATION TIME: 50 minutes
BAKING TIME: 15 minutes

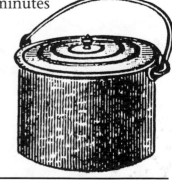

GOLDEN POTATO PUREE

*I **love** this dish — the color, the creamy texture, the taste. Sometimes when I boil potatoes, I add some cut up winter squash and mash the two together for a delicious combination.*

1 small- to medium-sized rutabaga, peeled and cut in eighths

3 medium potatoes, peeled and cut in halves

6 tablespoons butter

1 medium onion, finely chopped

1 teaspoon salt

3/4 teaspoon paprika

Black pepper

1. Cook both vegetables in separate pots of boiling water until fork tender.

2. While they are cooking, melt butter in a small skillet. Add onions and cook gently until translucent. Do not brown. Add salt, pepper, and paprika.

3. Drain potatoes and rutabagas. Put through a food mill together with onions.

4. Serve in a warmed vegetable dish. Sprinkle with additional paprika if desired.

YIELD: 6 servings

PREPARATION TIME: 30 minutes

WINTRY POTATO CASSEROLE

This casserole has warmed my family on many cold winter evenings. Try mixing potatoes with sliced, cooked turnips or carrots for a change of pace. If you substitute low-fat cottage cheese or yogurt, mix it with one tablespoon cornstarch to reduce any liquid separation.

6 large potatoes, peeled, boiled, sliced ¼" thick

2 cups cottage cheese

1 cup low-fat sour cream

2 cloves garlic, minced

2 shallots, finely chopped

Salt and pepper

3 plum tomatoes, sliced

¼ cup homemade bread crumbs

¼ cup cheese, Swiss, Parmesan, or combination

1. Preheat oven to 350 degrees.

2. Mix cottage cheese, sour cream, garlic, and shallots. Season with salt and pepper.

3. Add potatoes and stir to combine.

4. Place in shallow, buttered baking dish. Layer tomatoes on top.

5. Sprinkle with bread crumbs and cheese.

6. Bake for about 30 minutes.

YIELD: 4–6 servings
PREPARATION TIME: 30 minutes
COOKING TIME: 30 minutes

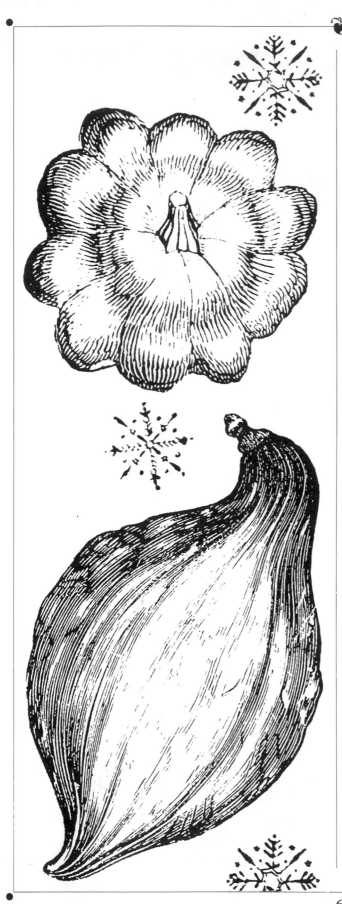

GINGER & GARLIC WINTER SQUASH

At Uphill Farm, we loved this vegetable dish as a delicious change from the usual maple-sweetened winter squash recipes. Winter squash stores well, so we usually had some in the cellar straight through 'til spring.

2 pounds squash (acorn, butternut, or buttercup)

1 cup water to cover

1 chicken or vegetable bouillon cube

1 tablespoon butter

2 tablespoons ginger, freshly chopped

4 cloves garlic, minced

1. Peel and chop squash into 1/2" pieces.

2. Boil in water flavored with bouillon cube and butter for 6–8 minutes, or until just tender.

3. Drain squash, reserving syrupy liquid.

4. Return liquid to pot, add ginger and garlic, and boil. Reduce liquid by half.

5. Return squash to saucepan and coat with liquid.

YIELD: 6 servings
COOKING TIME: 15 minutes

SAVORY PIES, STEWS, & ONE–DISH SUPPERS

Pizza Rustica

Cauliflower & Stilton Cheese Flan

Gougère with Artichoke Hearts & Feta Cheese

The Narrows Fish Stew

Country Paella

Lamb & Zucchini Stew with Lemon Sauce

Country Chicken Pie

An Uphill Cassoulet

Wild Mushroom Lasagne

Oyster Stew

A Beef Stew Provençal

Sausage & Cheese Soufflé

Potatoes Au Gratin with Leeks & Ham

Ragoût of Veal & Artichokes

Poule Au Pot

Babootie

PIZZA RUSTICA

This is a double-crusted, deep dish pizza. Truly a country dish, it benefits from the creative use of any on-hand ingredients or a fanciful raid of your garden. Your imagination and options will give Pizza Rustica its character. You may just hit upon the ultimate combination. Served with a green salad, it is a hearty, fun, and satisfying meal.

1 9" double pastry crust, your own (see page 114) or frozen

1 tablespoon butter or margarine, softened to room temperature

3 eggs

1 cup low-fat ricotta cheese

1/2 pound part-skim mozzarella cheese, cut in small cubes

1 cup plum tomatoes, drained, chopped, and drained again

1/2 cup freshly grated Parmesan cheese

2–3 cups filling options: mushrooms, ham pieces, sausage, zucchini, black or green olives, pimento, broccoli, cheeses, spinach, red or green peppers, fresh herbs

1. Preheat oven to 375 degrees.

2. Prepare pastry and fit into bottom of a 9" deep dish, spread with 1 tablespoon butter or margarine.

3. Beat eggs and ricotta until creamy. Stir in remaining ingredients, including filling options.

4. Spoon into pastry. Cover with top crust. Trim and crimp edges.

5. Bake 45 minutes. Allow to cool for 10 minutes before serving.

YIELD: 4–6 servings
PREPARATION TIME: Under 30 minutes, excluding crust
BAKING TIME: 45 minutes

CAULIFLOWER & STILTON CHEESE FLAN

One December, friends visiting from Ireland introduced me to Stilton cheese. It was their house gift to us, and I made this savory flan for the special occasion.

2 tablespoons butter or margarine

1 onion, chopped

2 tablespoons flour

3/4 cup milk

Pepper

1 pound cauliflower, cut in florets

1/4 pound Stilton cheese

1/4 cup grated cheese (cheddar, Jack, or Swiss)

1. Preheat oven to 375 degrees.

2. Melt butter in a pan and cook onions gently until soft. Stir in 2 tablespoons flour, stirring for 2 minutes over the heat.

3. With the pan off the heat, add milk gradually.

4. Bring to a boil, stirring, and continue to cook until sauce thickens. Season with pepper.

5. Arrange cauliflower in quiche pan. Sprinkle Stilton around and between florets.

6. Spoon the white sauce over cauliflower, and sprinkle on the grated cheese.

7. Bake 30 minutes or until golden and bubbly. Slice into pieces and serve.

YIELD: 6 servings

COOKING TIME: 40 minutes

VARIATION: Fill a partially baked pie crust (see page 114) with the above mixture for a cauliflower quiche.

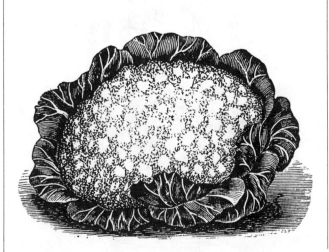

Gougère with Artichoke Hearts & Feta Cheese

I fondly remember the balmy evening when we ate this by the stone wall garden. The sun was setting and the air was becoming cooler. We drank wine until it grew dark, watched fireflies, and loved summer even more.

FILLING

3 tablespoons butter or margarine

1 tablespoon olive oil

1 leek, white part only, chopped

1 tablespoon flour

Salt and pepper

$1/2$ cup white wine

$1/2$ cup chicken or vegetable broth

1 teaspoon tomato paste, optional

1 tablespoon lemon juice

$8 1/2$ ounces artichoke hearts, canned or frozen and thawed

1 tomato, peeled

6–8 black olives, optional

4 ounces feta cheese

PÂTE À CHOUX

1 cup sifted flour

Salt and pepper

1 cup water

$1/2$ cup butter or margarine, cut in 3 pieces

4 eggs, room temperature

2 tablespoons freshly grated Parmesan cheese

TOPPING

$1/3$ cup grated Parmesan cheese

Fresh parsley

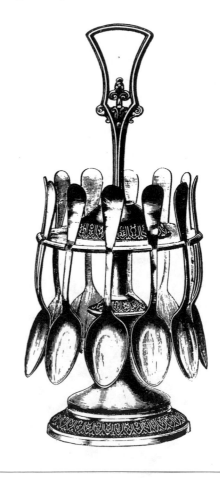

1. To prepare the filling, heat the butter and olive oil in a large skillet.

2. Split white part of leek in half, carefully washing out the grit. Cut in thin slices.

3. Heat the leeks in butter until softened. Do not brown.

4. Stir in the flour, salt, and pepper and continue cooking and stirring for 2 minutes.

5. Add wine, broth, tomato paste, and lemon juice. Bring to a boil and simmer 4 minutes. Remove from heat.

6. Cut peeled tomato in half and remove seeds with your fingers. Cut each half into 8 slices. Add to the leek mixture.

7. Halve each artichoke heart and add along with the olives. Set aside the filling and the feta cheese.

8. Preheat oven to 400 degrees.

9. To prepare pâte à choux, sift flour, salt, and pepper onto a paper plate or sheet of waxed paper.

10. Put water and butter in a large saucepan. Heat until the butter melts; then raise heat until the mixture boils.

11. Add flour *all at once* and stir continuously until the mixture draws away from the sides of the pan into a ball. Remove pan from heat. Cool for 5 minutes.

12. Add eggs, one at a time, and beat very well after each addition with a wooden spoon. Stir in Parmesan cheese.

13. Butter a 10" or 11" quiche or flan pan, or a baking dish. Spoon pastry mixture into a ring around the edges of the baking dish.

14. Pour the filling into the middle of your ring. With the wooden spoon, push back *pâte à choux* if it tends to slide toward the middle.

15. Break off the feta cheese into walnut-sized pieces; place throughout the filling. Sprinkle Parmesan topping over all.

16. Bake for 35–40 minutes. Gougère will puff and brown, and filling will be bubbly when done. Sprinkle with freshly snipped parsley and serve immediately.

YIELD: 6 servings
PREPARATION TIME: 35 minutes
BAKING TIME: 40 minutes

THE NARROWS FISH STEW

I generally couldn't bear to leave the hillside and farm in summer. I'd worry about missing peas, or harvesting beans. The ocean is my only competition for home. We usually go to the Narrows, a stretch of ocean in Maine, for one week in summer. Owen makes this fish stew every year while we are there. We look forward to it.

2 tablespoons olive oil

2 onions, chopped

4 cloves garlic, minced

1 rib of celery, chopped

2 tomatoes, peeled and chopped, or 8-ounce can of plum tomatoes

2 cups dry white wine

3 cups fish stock or 2 cups clam juice and 1 cup water

2 tablespoons chopped parsley

1 bay leaf

1 2" strip of orange peel, optional

10–15 mussels (well-cleaned in several changes of water)

$1/4$ cup white wine

1 teaspoon tarragon

$1^1/2$ pounds available white fish, cut in 1" pieces (cod, haddock, bass, monkfish)

$1/2$ pound scallops

4–6 crushed peppercorns

1 tablespoon Pernod, optional

AIOLI

1 clove garlic, minced

1 egg yolk

Pinch salt

$1/4$ cup olive oil

Salt and pepper

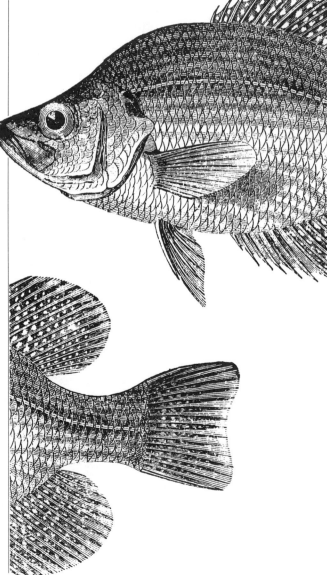

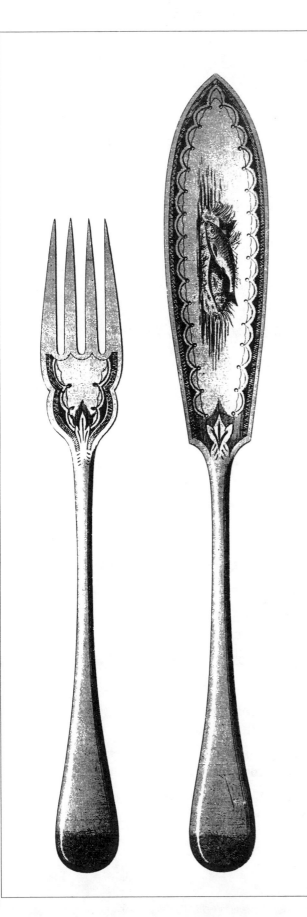

1. Lightly saute onions, garlic, and celery in olive oil until soft, but not browned.

2. Add tomatoes, 2 cups wine, and stock. Stir in parsley, bay leaf, and orange peel. Simmer for 30 minutes.

3. Simmer the mussels in an additional 1/4 cup of wine for approximately 6 minutes. Remove with a slotted spoon. Discard any unopened mussels. Remove mussels from shells. Strain cooking broth through cheesecloth.

4. Stir the white fish and scallops into the tomato-wine sauce, and add the tarragon, peppercorns, and Pernod.

5. Cook until the fish and scallops turn opaque, about 4 or 5 minutes. Do not overcook or fish will toughen.

6. Add mussels and strained mussel broth to the stew.

7. To prepare the sauce, beat the garlic, egg yolk, and a pinch of salt together in a separate bowl. Very slowly add olive oil, almost a drop at a time, while whisking continuously until incorporated.

8. A tablespoon of this sauce may be dolloped on top of each serving, or beat 2 tablespoons of the hot stew liquid into the sauce and then add all the sauce to the stew pot. Stir until well incorporated and season with salt and pepper.

YIELD: 8 servings
PREPARATION TIME: 45 minutes

COUNTRY PAELLA

The combination of farm food — our chickens, sausage, tomatoes, vegetables — and the sea has always appealed to me. This dish is a special occasion summer meal I've made for celebrating birthdays, Davy's state championships, or visiting relatives. Serve it outside on the porch or under a tree, leaving the heat of the kitchen and the day behind.

1/4 cup olive oil

2 tablespoons butter or margarine

3 pounds chicken, cut in small pieces

Flour

Salt

Pepper

3 onions, medium-sized, coarsely chopped

1/2 teaspoon oregano

1/4 cup chopped parsley

2 cloves garlic, minced

1 teaspoon salt

1/2 teaspoon freshly ground black pepper

1 red or yellow pepper, sliced

4 cups chicken or vegetable broth

4 tablespoons butter or margarine

2 cups rice

1 teaspoon saffron

Water or wine

3 tomatoes, peeled and cut into wedges

1/4 cup green or black olives

1 can artichoke hearts, drained and quartered

2 pimentos, chopped

1 chorizo sausage, sliced

18–24 medium shrimp, cooked and shelled

18–24 mussels or clams, scrubbed and cooked until shells open

Garnishes: parsley, pimentos, or pepper strips

1. Dust chicken in flour, salt, and pepper.

2. In a large skillet, saute chicken in hot oil and 2 tablespoons butter until golden.

3. Add onions and stir to color. Stir in parsley, oregano, garlic, salt, and pepper.

4. Add red or yellow pepper and broth to cover. Simmer, covered over low heat until chicken is tender, about 25–30 minutes.

5. Pour liquid from skillet and reserve. Set chicken mixture aside.

6. Melt butter in saucepan. Add rice and cook, stirring until rice yellows. Stir in saffron.

7. Pour in reserved broth from chicken and additional wine or liquid to total 4 cups. Simmer over low heat until liquid is absorbed, about 25 minutes.

8. Combine rice, chicken, tomatoes, olives, artichoke hearts, pimentos, and sliced sausage in paella pan or large, shallow oven dish.

9. Cook covered in 350 degree oven for 20 minutes.

10. Remove from oven, then tuck shrimp and opened shellfish around the top. Season with additional pepper and continue cooking for 10 minutes more.

11. Remove from oven. Garnish the top as you wish.

YIELD: 8 servings

PREPARATION TIME: 1 hour

COOKING TIME: 45 minutes

VARIATIONS: Anything can be added to this delicious dish. Use rice as the foundation. Try peas, summer squash, lobster, or any meat for substitutes. It is possible to prepare this a day ahead for company. Prepare through step 8 the day before. Before serving, stir while reheating rice mixture. Bring liquids to a boil and add to heated rice. Proceed.

Lamb & Zucchini Stew with Lemon Sauce

Even though we kept a full chest freezer of vegetables and fruit, we also shared a freezer locker in town. "Going to the locker" usually meant we'd have a meal of lamb, pork, or beef, as this was where we stored most of our meats. The seasoned lamb and lemony sauce give the stew its a robust flavor. Serve with a simple parsley rice, warmed French bread with sweet butter, and a good, red Bourdeaux.

1/4 cup olive oil

2 pounds boneless shoulder of lamb, cut in 1" cubes

1 large onion, chopped

2 cloves garlic, minced

Salt and pepper

2 cups water

2 medium zucchini, or 3 small

SAUCE

3 eggs

Juice of 2 lemons

1 3/4 cups pan drippings from cooked lamb (approximate)

Salt and pepper

Chopped parsley

1. Heat the oil in a stew pot. Brown the lamb with onion and garlic. Season with salt and pepper.

2. Add water and simmer for 1 1/2 hours.

3. Cut zucchini in 1/2"-thick slices. Add to the lamb. Simmer for 10 minutes more, or until meat is tender.

4. Remove meat and zucchini with a slotted spoon to a dish, reserving cooking liquid, and keep warm while you prepare the sauce.

5. Beat the three eggs until foamy. Slowly add lemon juice, while you continue beating.

6. Gradually add the cooking liquid from the cooked lamb, beating until slightly thickened.

7. Pour the sauce over the lamb and zucchini. Season with salt and pepper. Garnish with parsley. Serve hot.

YIELD: 6 servings

PREPARATION TIME: 15 minutes

COOKING TIME: 1 1/2 hours

VARIATION: Change or mix vegetables: broccoli, green beans, and cauliflower would all be good with the lemony sauce.

COUNTRY CHICKEN PIE

I've always loved chicken pies, one of the all-time comforting foods for me. Warm from the oven, the meat and vegetables are creamy and fork-tender. Chicken Pie seems like such a relaxed dish to prepare, maybe because like chicken soup, it is hard to rush, or maybe because it only occurs to me to make it when I have the time to linger in the kitchen.

This version mixes the traditional tastes of pastry, gravy, and chicken with less traditional vegetables: mushrooms, pearl onions, and broccoli. You, of course, can vary the vegetables: artichoke hearts and leeks lend it new flavors; peas, carrots, celery, onions, turnips, and pimento make it downright homey.

¹/₂ cup pearl onions

4 tablespoons butter or margarine

12 mushrooms, quartered

6 tablespoons flour

1¹/₂ cups chicken broth

1 cup half-and-half

2 tablespoons Cognac or sherry

1¹/₂ cups cooked chicken, cut in bite-sized pieces

3/4 – 1 cup cooked broccoli or canned artichoke hearts, cut in small pieces

1 sheet frozen puff pastry, or your own pastry (see page 114)

1. First prepare the onions: Cut a shallow cross into the root end of each onion. Put onions in boiling water and simmer for 5 minutes. Remove with a slotted spoon and dip in cold water. Peel skins and set onions aside.

2. Melt butter in a skillet. Toss in mushrooms and saute for a few minutes. Whisk in flour and stir 3 minutes.

3. Pour in broth and half-and-half. Bring to a boil, stirring occasionally. Add Cognac or sherry; simmer until slightly thickened.

4. Preheat oven to 375 degrees.

5. Stir chicken, broccoli, and onions into cream sauce.

6. Pour chicken filling into a deep oven dish or casserole. Cut pastry the shape of casserole top with a 1" overhang.

7. Gently place pastry over the casserole with pastry overhanging casserole edges. Do not trim.

8. Bake for 30 minutes.

YIELD: 6 servings
PREPARATION TIME: 40 minutes
BAKING TIME: 30 minutes

AN UPHILL CASSOULET

*Cassoulet is a traditional French baked bean dish. Many include **confite d'oie** (preserved goose) or duck, mutton, pork, ham, sausage, bacon. Using beans and broth as a base, it is easy to create individual versions. We had venison in the fall at Uphill, given to us by the men who hunted in the upper hillside. Venison, as well as bits of available meat (sausage, lamb, chicken, duck) will enrich this dish. Serve it in the dish it is prepared in; an earthenware dish is traditional.*

1½ – 2 pounds dried white beans, soaked overnight, in cold water to cover

2 onions, chopped

½ teaspoon salt

¼ teaspoon dried thyme

1 bay leaf

1 tablespoon chopped parsley

1 pound pork link or turkey sausage

½ pound lean salt pork

4 tablespoons fat (pork trimmings, butter, or margarine)

2 pounds boned shoulder or leg of lamb, cut in 1" cubes

2 cloves garlic, minced

½ teaspoon salt

2 tablespoons tomato paste

Freshly ground black pepper

1 clove garlic, split

2 tablespoons chopped parsley

1 cup fresh bread crumbs

2–3 tablespoons butter or margarine

1. Soak beans overnight and drain. Put in a large saucepan and cover with cold water.

2. Add onions, salt, thyme, bay leaf, parsley, sausage, and salt pork.

3. Bring to a boil and simmer for 30 minutes. Remove sausage and continue to simmer for 1 hour longer.

4. Meanwhile, in a large skillet, melt butter or fat. Add lamb, the minced garlic, and salt. Cook until lamb browns lightly.

5. Add some liquid from the bean pot to cover the lamb. Mix in tomato paste and pepper. Simmer for about 1 hour. Meanwhile, stir and add additional liquid to the beans as needed.

6. Preheat oven to 300 degrees.

7. Drain beans, reserving liquid.

8. Remove salt pork and cut in small 1/2" cubes. Slice sausage in 1/2" pieces.

9. Combine sausage, salt pork, and lamb and set aside.

10. Rub a large earthenware casserole with the split clove of garlic.

11. Put a third of the beans in the dish. Next, add half the meat, another third of beans, the remaining meat, then the remaining beans.

12. Pour in juices from the lamb skillet and enough bean liquid to cover. Bake, covered, for 1 hour.

13. Uncover, add a bit more bean liquid, if needed to almost cover and sprinkle with bread crumbs and parsley. Dot with 2–3 tablespoons of butter.

14. Return to oven, uncovered, for an additional 30 minutes or so. Topping should be brown and crusty. Serve from the casserole.

YIELD: 8–10 servings

COOKING TIME: 4 1/2 hours

VARIATIONS: This is a country dish; don't be afraid to try your own versions using meats you have available — leftover poultry, venison, pork chops, sausage patties, or ham hocks, layered among the beans. White wine or vermouth can be used for part of the lamb braising liquid in step five.

WILD MUSHROOM LASAGNE

I can never have enough prepare-ahead recipes. This is one such recipe that works well in advance — just save the baking for the day it is to be served. The mushrooms, cheese, and prosciutto mix together for a hearty, flavorful meal.

1/4 cup olive oil

4 tablespoons butter or margarine

2 pounds mushroom mixture (shiitake, porcini, or fresh domestic), coarsely chopped

3 tablespoons sherry

1 onion, finely chopped

1 (14 1/2-ounce) can plum tomatoes, drained and chopped

1/4 cup flat Italian parsley, finely chopped

Salt and pepper

1 pound lasagna noodles

8 tablespoons plus 2 teaspoons butter or margarine

1/3 cup flour

4 ounces milk

1/4 pound Parmesan cheese

1/4 pound prosciutto, thinly sliced

8 ounces mozzarella cheese, grated

1. In large skillet, heat oil and 4 tablespoons butter; add mushrooms and cook until liquid is released and evaporated.

2. Add sherry and cook until absorbed.

3. Add onion, tomatoes, and parsley. Cook for 5 minutes.

4. Cook pasta in 4 quarts of boiling water for 5–7 minutes. Drain, rinse in cold water.

5. Preheat oven to 425 degrees.

6. Melt remaining butter in saucepan. Gradually add flour and stir for 4 minutes.

7. Slowly add milk. Whisk until thick and smooth. Season with salt and pepper.

8. Butter lasagne pan. Layer pasta, then 1/3 of mushroom mix, then 1/4 sauce. Sprinkle Parmesan cheese on the sauce, then place pieces of prosciutto on this. Repeat layering twice more. Over top of the pasta, spoon the remaining sauce, mozzarella, and Parmesan. Dot with butter.

10. Bake 25 minutes. Allow to cool and set for 10 minutes.

YIELD: 12 servings

PREPARATION TIME: 20 minutes

COOKING TIME: 30 minutes

VARIATION: For a vegetarian meal, omit the prosciutto and substitute with 1 cup steamed chopped spinach, drained well. Add 2 cloves garlic to the sauce for more flavor.

OYSTER STEW

On Christmas Eve, we joined Owen's parents and siblings at Wild farm. With a fire in the living room, we ate this creamy oyster stew and Sally Lunn bread. This stew is simple — perfect given the busy nature of the day. After dinner, we lit the candles on the tree and sang carols.

4 tablespoons butter

1/4 teaspoon Worcestershire sauce

2 cups shucked oysters, juices reserved

2 cups milk

2 cups light cream

Salt

Butter

Paprika

1. Melt butter until bubbly. Stir in Worcestershire sauce.

2. Add oysters and cook gently, swirling the pan for almost 2 minutes. The oysters' edges should just begin to curl.

3. Add milk, cream, and reserved juices. Cook until it barely simmers.

4. Add salt to taste.

5. Spoon into four hot soup bowls. Melt a bit of butter on top and sprinkle with paprika if desired.

YIELD: 4–5 servings

PREPARATION TIME: 5 minutes

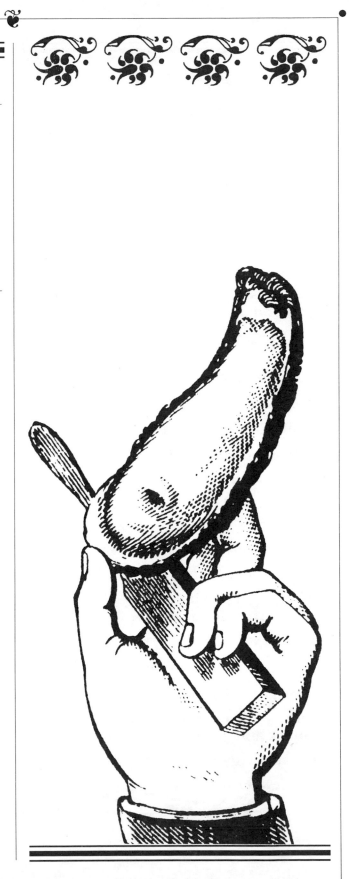

A Beef Stew Provençal

Winter weekends brought a slower pace — something we were all ready for. It was a time when we could linger over the Sunday paper, listen to music, and catch up on projects. We took more time with preparing supper, too, often cooking dishes that would simmer on the stove as we played a game of cards or charades.

¹/3 cup parsley

2 cloves garlic

Freshly ground black pepper

1 tablespoon olive oil

2 slices bacon

2 pounds beef stew meat, fat trimmed and cut in 1¹/2" cubes

2 tablespoons flour

2 tablespoons brandy

1¹/2 cups white wine
(use red wine for a heartier flavor)

¹/2 cup water

2 teaspoons tomato paste

¹/4 teaspoon thyme

20 pitted olives, a combination of black and green

Salt and pepper

1. Mince together parsley, garlic, and black pepper.

2. Cut uncooked bacon into 2" pieces. Cook with olive oil in a large casserole over low heat until bacon begins to render its fat and browns. Remove bacon with slotted spoon.

3. Coat stew beef in the parsley mixture.

4. Raise heat and brown the meat in the bacon fat on all sides.

5. Add the flour, and stir gently for 2 minutes.

6. Pour in the brandy, wine, and water. Stir in the tomato paste, and thyme. Cover and simmer for 1¹/2 hours.

7. Uncover. Add the olives for an additional ¹/2 hour of cooking. Season with salt and pepper.

YIELD: 6 servings

PREPARATION TIME: 30 minutes

COOKING TIME: 2 hours

VARIATION: Substitute (or add) mushrooms and pearl onions for the olives. Add after 1 hour of cooking. Add the flour to the parsley mixture before dredging the meat. After browning the meat, heat the brandy, ignite, and pour over the braised meat.

Sausage & Cheese Soufflé

It wasn't always planned ahead, but chances were fair that we would have a house full of company most weekends at Uphill. I often prepared this the night before for friends who stayed. It needs to be readied at least four hours before baking.

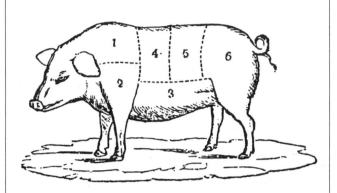

6 slices stale bread, white or a light whole wheat

2 tablespoons butter or margarine

1 pound good quality bulk pork or turkey sausage

1/4 pound sharp cheddar cheese, grated

2 eggs, well-beaten

1 1/2 teaspoons Dijon-style mustard

2 cups milk

1. Remove crusts and lightly butter the bread.

2. Cook sausage until brown. Drain if there is excessive fat.

3. In a buttered soufflé dish, alternate layers of bread, sausage, and cheese.

4. Mix together the eggs, mustard, and milk. Pour over the layered bread, and let stand at least 4 hours or overnight. Return to room temperature prior to baking.

5. Preheat oven to 375 degrees. Bake 45 minutes and serve immediately.

YIELD: 4–6 servings

PREPARATION TIME: 30 minutes

REFRIGERATION TIME: 4 hours or overnight

BAKING TIME: 45 minutes

POTATOES AU GRATIN WITH LEEKS & HAM

*Old French cooking books were added to Uphill's kitchen. Basic recipes were practiced, **bonne femme**-style, — fluffy omelets, creamy soups, and gratins — using the foods in season or on hand to produce very good, very efficient home cooking.*

4 medium to large potatoes, peeled and sliced 1/4" thick

2 cups milk

Pinch nutmeg, salt, and pepper

4 tablespoons butter or margarine

2 leeks, white part only, split and rinsed

1 clove garlic, minced

8-ounce ham slice, 1/4" thick, cut in 1" pieces

1 1/2 cups grated Swiss cheese

2 tablespoons half-and-half

2 tablespoons grated Parmesan cheese

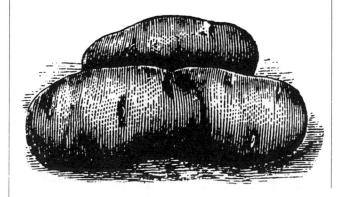

1. Bring milk, salt, pepper, and nutmeg to a simmer. Add potatoes and cook 15 minutes or until tender.

2. Melt 2 tablespoons of the butter in a skillet. Add leeks and garlic; stir over medium-low heat to soften leeks. Add ham, raise heat, and stir for 2 minutes more.

3. Heat oven to 400 degrees.

4. Lightly butter an oval ceramic or enamel baking dish. Spread a thin layer of ham and leeks, then cut potatoes in half. Sprinkle on more pepper and half of the grated Swiss cheese. Layer the rest of the ham, then the remaining potatoes. Sprinkle more pepper and the remaining Swiss cheese.

5. Pour the half-and-half over all. Dot with the remaining butter and add the grated Parmesan cheese.

6. Bake for 30 minutes until browned and bubbly.

YIELD: 4 servings
PREPARATION TIME: 20 minutes
BAKING TIME: 30 minutes

Ragoût of Veal & Artichokes

We were able to do a lot of bartering at the farm. Owen traded raw milk and yogurt, syrup, eggs, and cider for other foods, including veal. When you can get good local veal, this is a lovely dish in which to use it. I like it served with rice.

Olive oil

3 onions, chopped

3 cloves garlic, minced

2 1/2 – 3 pounds veal stew meat, cut in 1 1/2" to 2" cubes

3 tablespoons flour

1 1/2 cups beef broth

3/4 – 1 cup white wine

Juice of 1 lemon

2 tablespoons tomato paste

1 bay leaf

1/2 teaspoon rosemary

Pinch thyme

Freshly ground black pepper

3/4 pound mushrooms, sliced

1 package frozen artichoke hearts, partially defrosted, or 1 can, drained

1/4 cup black olives, optional

Grated lemon peel, optional

1/4 cup finely chopped parsley

1. Heat 2 tablespoons olive oil in a large skillet. Saute the onions and garlic until translucent. Transfer to a 5-quart Dutch oven or enamel stove-top casserole with a lid.

2. Add another 2 tablespoons olive oil to the large skillet and brown the veal, a few pieces at a time, over medium-high heat. Add to Dutch oven. Continue browning veal, adding more oil as needed.

3. Lower heat under skillet. Add 2 tablespoons oil and the flour, stirring to make a paste. Add broth, wine, and the juice of 1 lemon. Stir up brown bits from the bottom of the pan. Add tomato paste, bay leaf, rosemary, thyme, and pepper. Simmer for 5 minutes.

4. Pour this sauce over the veal in the Dutch oven. Cover and cook for 1 hour.

5. Uncover and continue cooking for 50 minutes more, stirring frequently.

6. Add the sliced mushrooms to the skillet. Cover and cook over medium-high heat for 2 minutes; uncover and stir until liquid has evaporated.

7. Add the sauteed mushrooms, along with the artichoke hearts, black olives, and lemon peel to the Dutch oven. Simmer for 10 more minutes.

8. Ten minutes before serving, add the parsley to the ragout, and reheat.

YIELD: 8 servings
PREPARATION TIME: 25 minutes
COOKING TIME: 2 hours 15 minutes

POULE AU POT

I've seen many versions of poule au pot. Sometimes the chicken is stuffed with rice. Like most simply prepared food, this is only as good as its individual ingredients. Try to use free-range chicken and a good, homemade broth, if possible.

1 whole roasting chicken
($2^{1}/_2$–3 pounds), rinsed and wiped dry

4 cups chicken broth

$^{1}/_2$ cup white wine, vermouth, or dry sherry

1 bay leaf

$^{1}/_4$ teaspoon thyme

1 whole clove garlic

3 carrots, trimmed into 1",
oval-shaped pieces

3 small turnips, cut into $^{1}/_2$" wedges

3 leeks, white part scrubbed and sliced into 1" pieces

2 parsnips, sliced on a diagonal,
$^{1}/_2$" thick

1. Tie chicken legs together and place breast side down in saucepan just big enough to hold the bird.

2. Pour broth and wine over chicken; add bay leaf, thyme, and garlic. Bring to a simmer over low heat. Cover and poach for 1 hour.

3. Turn chicken over. Spread carrots, turnips, leeks, and parsnips around chicken. Cover and continue cooking (do not boil) for 15 minutes more. Check chicken for doneness.

4. Remove chicken to platter.

5. Continue cooking vegetables 5 minutes more, skimming foam from surface.

6. Divide vegetables among 4 warm, shallow soup bowls. Thinly slice breast meat and place over vegetables. Ladle broth over all.

YIELD: 4 servings
COOKING TIME: 45 minutes

BABOOTIE

I first had this dish while in college at potluck suppers. What makes it special is its slightly sweet, curried flavor. At Uphill Farm, I used our ground lamb instead of the beef from the college version. It was a big hit!

2 pounds lean ground lamb, beef, or turkey

2 onions, grated

2 cloves garlic, minced

16 ounces tomatoes

1½ tablespoons granulated sugar

2 tablespoons curry powder

2 tablespoons cider vinegar

Pinch salt

2 firm bananas

1 apple, peeled and chopped

1 tablespoon apricot jam

Garnishes

1. Brown meat in a large skillet; drain off the fat.

2. Add the remaining ingredients, breaking up bananas with a wooden spoon.

3. Cover and simmer gently for 30 minutes.

4. Serve hot with rice or buttered noodles. Pass bowls of peanuts, flaked coconut, raisins, and your favorite chutney.

YIELD: 8 servings

PREPARATION TIME: Under 30 minutes

COOKING TIME: 30 minutes

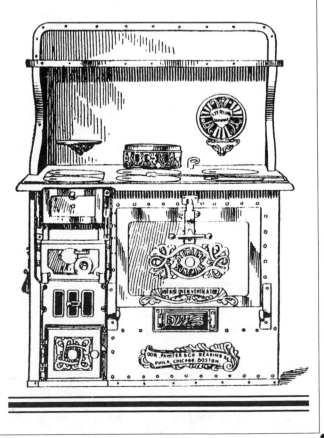

COUNTRY SUPPERS *for* FAMILY & FRIENDS

Mushrooms & Pasta Baked with Two Cheeses

Two Roast Chickens

Pan-Fried Catfish with Spicy Red Sauce

Linguine in Herbed Artichoke Sauce

Ham in Tarragon Cream Sauce

Orange Rice & Chicken with Almonds

Autumn Pork Supper

Filled Biscuits

Crumbed Chicken in Wine Sauce

Hot Stuffed Italian Bread

Creamed Chicken with Vermont Corn Bread

Lamb Medallions with Potato Parmesan Crust

Tortellini in a Sausage Cream Sauce

Garnishes

MUSHROOMS & PASTA BAKED WITH TWO CHEESES

A blend of ribbon noodles in a thick, cheese-based sauce gives this pasta dish its wonderful aroma and flavor. Serve with a green salad, and pears or red grapes for dessert.

8 ounces wide or ribbon noodles

2 tablespoons butter or margarine

2 cloves garlic, minced

8–10 ounces mushrooms, domestic or mixed wild, sliced

2 ounces Gorgonzola or Stilton cheese, crumbled

5 tablespoons half-and-half (may substitute 2 tablespoons milk for 2 tablespoons of the half-and-half)

Salt and pepper

1 egg, beaten

4 ounces part-skim mozzarella cheese

1. Preheat oven to 350 degrees.

2. Cook noodles until tender. Drain.

3. Melt butter. Cook garlic and mushrooms, stirring frequently until softened.

4. Stir in crumbled Gorgonzola cheese, and cook until melted.

5. Stir in cream, and season with salt and pepper.

6. Season noodles with pepper. Mix with mushroom sauce and egg.

7. Turn into a buttered oven dish. Grate mozzarella on top. Cover with foil, and bake for 10 minutes.

8. Uncover, set oven to 425 degrees, and continue cooking for 10–15 minutes.

YIELD: 4 servings

PREPARATION TIME: 15 minutes

COOKING TIME: 25 minutes

VARIATIONS: Instead of baking, omit the egg and toss the warm pasta with the mushroom cream sauce. A milder cheese like a garlic herb cream cheese can be substituted for the Gorgonzola.

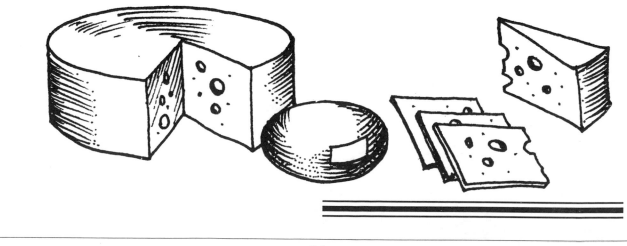

Two Roast Chickens

Roast chickens are my favorite meal of all. In winter, I roast chicken with stuffing, serve with warm biscuits or corn bread, and make a cider-flavored gravy. In summer, roast chicken becomes a different sort of treat. Cook it in the early cool of the day, the cavity filled with sprigs of herbs and garlic. Serve it later with bread, Hungarian Rice Salad (see page 33), and wine. It's a light, flavorful supper that we often carried to a table set out in the orchard.

Roasting Chicken

There are many approaches to roasting a chicken - breast side up, down, or both; rack or not, truss or not; covered with foil at beginning, at end of roasting, or not at all; oven temperature 325 degrees all the way to 450 degrees; basted with butter, water, or not basted at all. Use any technique that yields good results for you. The important thing is not to overcook it — dried out chicken is a disaster. The meat is finished cooking when the thigh joint moves easily, or the meat feels soft when squeezed. Juices will run out clear, not pink.

In the following recipes, I use a 350 degree oven for about 22 minutes per pound. I baste frequently. Flavor the meat by filling the cavity with salt, pepper, onions, garlic, parsley, and available herbs or fruits.

LEMON ROASTED CHICKEN

2 1/2 – 3 1/2 pound roasting chicken

Salt and pepper

1 lemon, halved

1 clove garlic

1/2 onion or 1 shallot

Sprig of parsley

Sprig of thyme, optional

Butter or oil

GRAVY

1 tablespoon flour

1 1/4 cups chicken broth

1/4 cup white wine or vermouth

1 tablespoon lemon juice

Salt and pepper

1. Preheat oven to 350 degrees.

2. Prepare chicken by cutting the fat from its cavity and removing the giblets. Rinse in cool water and dry with paper towels, inside and out.

3. Salt and pepper inside of chicken. Squeeze in juice of 1/2 lemon and then place the lemon in the cavity. Also add onion or shallot, garlic, and sprigs of parsley and thyme.

4. Rub outside of chicken with salt, pepper, and butter or oil. Place meat, breast side down, in a shallow pan. Do not use a rack.

5. Baste after 20 minutes with accumulated pan juices or lemon juice and water mixture.

6. After 10 more minutes, baste again and turn the chicken breast side up for the remaining basting and cooking.

7. Roast for 20–25 minutes per pound. The thigh joint should move easily up and down, and the juices run clear when done.

8. When chicken is ready, transfer to a platter. Serve when meat cools to room temperature (most flavorful) or refrigerate for serving later. Allow to return to room temperature before serving.

9. For serving warm with gravy: Pour off all but 2 tablespoons of drippings in pan. Heat them (in roaster) on top of stove. Add 1 tablespoon flour and stir with a wire whisk. Stir in broth and wine. Bring to a boil and simmer until slightly reduced and thickened. Squeeze in remaining lemon juice. Add salt and pepper to taste.

YIELD: 4–6 servings

PREPARATION TIME: 15 minutes

ROASTING TIME: About 1 hour

BASIL CHICKEN

Make this at the end of summer, when you want a change from pesto and your fresh basil supply is still plentiful.

2¹/₂–3 pound roasting chicken

1 small bunch chives, snipped, or 1 shallot

1 generous bunch fresh basil

Olive oil

Salt and pepper

1. Preheat oven to 350 degrees.

2. Remove fat from cavity. Rinse chicken in cool water and pat dry with paper towels, inside and out.

3. Salt and pepper cavity. Add the chives or shallot, and generous bunch of basil leaves. Reserve 8 leaves.

4. Rub olive oil and salt over outside of bird.

5. Place chicken, breast side down, in a shallow pan. Do not use a rack. Baste after 20 minutes with pan juices. After 10 more minutes, baste again and remove from oven.

6. Turn chicken breast side up. Arrange basil leaves in a pattern over breast. Affix these with a thin coating of olive oil.

7. Return to oven and continue roasting and basting until done, about 20–25 minutes per pound or until thigh joint moves easily, and juices run clear.

8. Place chicken on platter. Serve warm or at room temperature with pan juices.

YIELD: 4–6 servings
PREPARATION TIME: 15 minutes
COOKING TIME: About 1 hour

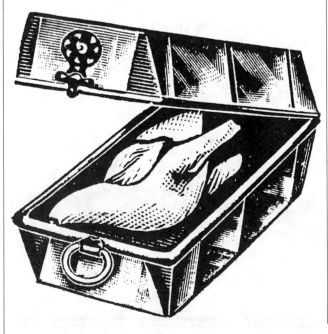

Pan-Fried Catfish with Spicy Red Sauce

This spicy catfish recipe is just the right choice for dinner on hurried evenings. It cooks up quickly and the sauce can be made up, and even frozen, ahead of time.

CATFISH

4 (6-ounce) catfish fillets

3 tablespoons cornmeal

1 teaspoon chili powder

1/2 teaspoon paprika

Freshly ground black pepper

Olive oil

SPICY RED SAUCE

1/4 cup olive oil

2 cups chopped onion

1 cup chopped red or green pepper

1 cup chopped celery

2 cloves garlic, minced

2 1/4 pounds tomatoes, canned

6 ounces tomato paste

Salt and pepper to taste

1 tablespoon Worcestershire sauce

1 strip lemon rind

2 cloves

1/2 teaspoon sugar

1/2 teaspoon thyme

1/2 teaspoon rosemary

1 bay leaf

1/4 cup chopped parsley

2 drops Tabasco

1/2 teaspoon red pepper

1. Saute onion, peppers, celery, and garlic in the oil until the onion is translucent.

2. Add the tomatoes and remaining ingredients. Simmer for 15 minutes.

3. Mix cornmeal, chili powder, paprika, and pepper on waxed paper. Coat fish with mixture on both sides.

4. Heat olive oil to cover in another pan over medium high heat.

5. Fry catfish for about 4 minutes per side or until fish flakes easily. Spoon sauce on plate to the side of the fish.

YIELD: 4 servings

PREPARATION TIME: 25 minutes

COOKING TIME: 10 minutes

LINGUINE IN HERBED ARTICHOKE SAUCE

Tomatoes and wine are classic pasta sauce ingredients. Since we always had fresh cream, it, too, was added to many dishes. If you omit it, you'll still have a lovely sauce to toss with the linguine.

12–16 ounces linguine or similar light pasta

1 tablespoon butter or margarine

2 tablespoons olive oil

10 ounces mushrooms, wiped clean and sliced

1 onion, chopped

2 cloves garlic, minced

1/2 cup white wine

1 cup chicken or vegetable broth

Salt and pepper

1 tablespoon fresh basil, or 1 teaspoon dried

Pinch rosemary, optional

2 tablespoons chopped parsley

2 tablespoons tomato paste

1 (10-ounce) package frozen artichoke hearts, prepared according to directions, and quartered

1/2 cup half-and-half or light cream

1. Heat butter and oil in a skillet. Add mushrooms, onion, and garlic. Saute over low heat until tender; garlic and onion should not brown.

2. Raise heat. Add wine and broth. Stir until mixture comes to a boil. Stir in herbs, salt, pepper, and tomato paste. Simmer for about 5 minutes, stirring occasionally.

3. Add artichoke hearts. Cook gently for a few minutes more.

4. Cook pasta. Drain and put in a heated bowl or platter.

5. Stir the half-and-half into the sauce. Heat to almost boiling.

6. Toss sauce with pasta. Serve immediately with hot garlic bread.

YIELD: 4–6 servings
PREPARATION TIME: 10 minutes

HAM IN TARRAGON CREAM SAUCE

French tarragon is a pungent herb and I always try to have it growing in my garden. It's wonderful with chicken, and surprisingly good with this ham. Serve with crisp, sauteed, walnut-sized potatoes.

2 pounds cooked ham, sliced 1/3" thick

2 tablespoons butter or margarine

1 tablespoon oil

2 shallots, very finely chopped

1/2 teaspoon dried tarragon, or 1 1/2 teaspoons fresh

1 tablespoon flour

1/2 cup Madeira or vermouth

1 tablespoon Cognac, optional

1 tablespoon tarragon wine vinegar, or white wine vinegar

1 teaspoon tomato paste

1/2 teaspoon Dijon-style mustard

1/2 cup half-and-half

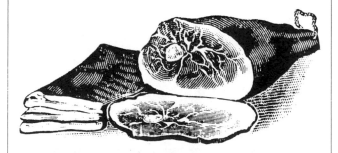

1. Dry ham slices with a paper towel. Trim off excess fat. Cut ham slices in 2 or 3 large pieces if meat is too large for skillet.

2. Add a piece of the trimmed fat to 1 tablespoon butter and oil in large skillet. When fat is hot, lightly brown ham on both sides. Transfer to a warm platter.

3. Drain most of the fat from the pan. Add the remaining 1 tablespoon butter, shallots, and tarragon. Cook over low heat for 1 minute.

4. Add flour; stir with a wire whisk for 2 minutes more.

5. Add Madeira and Cognac. Bring to a boil, then simmer for 5 minutes.

6. Blend vinegar, tomato paste, and mustard into the sauce. Continue to simmer, partially covered for 10 minutes more.

7. Add the cream to the skillet. Return to a simmer and allow to reduce slightly.

8. Return ham and any juices to the skillet. Heat through.

9. Spoon sauce over ham. Arrange ham on a serving platter and garnish with sprigs of tarragon or other greens.

YIELD: 4 servings

PREPARATION TIME: 30 minutes

VARIATION: Use light cream in place of the half-and-half for an even richer sauce.

ORANGE RICE & CHICKEN WITH ALMONDS

This sweet, citrus-flavored rice and chicken dish is a simple preparation. Serve it with steamed spinach or peas.

RICE

4 tablespoons butter or margarine

1 onion, chopped

2 1/2 cups rice

2 cups orange juice and water combination (dilute to taste)

2 cups water

1 teaspoon grated orange rind

2 teaspoons salt

1 tablespoon parsley

CHICKEN

4 tablespoons butter or margarine

1/2 cup sliced almonds

3 whole chicken breasts, cut in half (6 serving pieces)

Salt and pepper

1 cup water and orange juice combination

1. In a large saucepan, saute onion in butter until golden.

2. Add the rice and stir for a minute or two.

3. Add the remaining rice ingredients.

4. Bring to a boil, stir, cover, and simmer for 20 minutes until rice is fluffy.

5. Leave covered until serving.

6. While rice is cooking, saute almonds in 4 tablespoons butter in a large skillet. Remove almonds from skillet when golden brown, and set aside.

7. Rinse chicken breasts, and pat dry. Season with salt and pepper.

8. Brown (in same skillet that almonds were in) until golden brown. This should take 15–20 minutes. Remove from skillet.

9. Deglaze skillet with 1 cup of orange juice. Boil and reduce by half.

10. Fluff rice and place on a heated platter. Arrange chicken on top. Pour sauce over chicken and sprinkle with sauteed almonds. Garnish with orange slices.

YIELD: 4–6 servings
PREPARATION TIME: 15 minutes
COOKING TIME: 25 minutes

AUTUMN PORK SUPPER

This meal is a fine example of how supper can be created around seasonal ingredients: apples, cider, and cabbage, combined with pork.

CABBAGE

1 large cabbage, about 10 cups, coarsely chopped

2 tablespoons butter or margarine

2 cloves garlic, minced

1 medium onion, coarsely chopped

2 apples, cored and cut in eighths

Salt and pepper

PORK CHOPS

6 loin pork chops, $1/2$"–$3/4$" thick

3 tablespoons oil and butter combination

$1/2$ cup apple cider or juice

2 tablespoons brandy or calvados, optional

Salt and pepper

ASSEMBLY

1 bay leaf

2 tablespoons bread crumbs

2 tablespoons freshly grated Parmesan cheese

$1/2$ cup heated cider or light cream

1. Bring 2 inches of water to a boil in a large pot. Cook cabbage about 3 minutes. Drain.

2. In a large skillet, melt butter. Saute onion and garlic over low heat, stirring until translucent, not brown. Add apples and cabbage, and salt and pepper to taste. Stir for another 3 minutes. Set aside in a bowl.

3. Pat pork chops dry with a paper towel. Season with salt and pepper.

4. In the same skillet used for the apple-cabbage mixture, heat the oil and butter. When hot, add chops and brown for a few minutes on each side. Remove and set aside.

5. Add cider and brandy to deglaze pan. Boil rapidly and reduce liquid by half.

6. Pour this liquid over the cabbage mixture. Preheat oven to 350 degrees.

7. Use a covered, heavy, oven dish, large enough to hold a single layer of 3 chops. Spread 1/3 of the cabbage in the bottom of the dish; then layer 3 chops, then a second layer of cabbage, then second layer of chops. Finish with a layer of cabbage.

8. Lay bay leaf on top and sprinkle on bread crumbs and cheese. Pour optional cider or cream over all.

9. Bake, covered, for 30 minutes. Remove cover and bake an additional 5–10 minutes.

YIELD: 4–6 servings
PREPARATION TIME: 45 minutes
BAKING TIME: 40 minutes

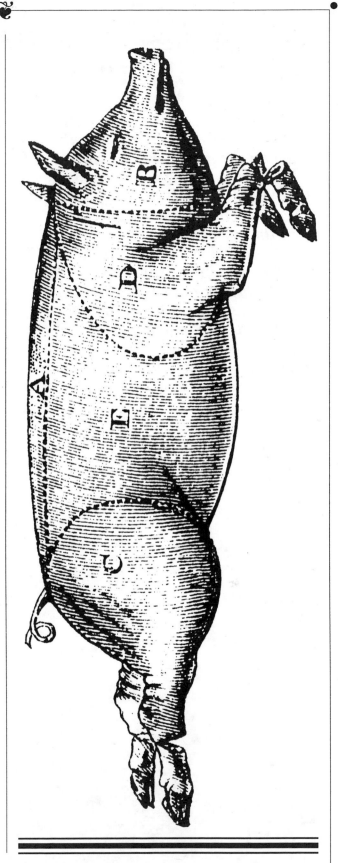

FILLED BISCUITS

These flaky biscuits are a simple version of Cornish pasties, a warm and filling lunch on the run. A trayful brought out to the barn was a welcome break during days long with cider-making or haying.

We still enjoy these biscuits warm from the oven with butter, adding salad or soup for a light supper. Although this is a tidy way to use small quantities of leftover pork roast (some of us get inspired not wasting even the tiniest bit), I have also made it using two uncooked pork chops. Cut chops into small pieces, saute meat with garlic, salt, and pepper, and then proceed with recipe.

2 cups flour

1 teaspoon salt

2^1/$_2$ teaspoons baking powder

4 tablespoons butter or margarine

^{1}/$_3$ cup milk

^{1}/$_3$ cup water

^{1}/$_2$ cup cooked, well-seasoned lean pork or chicken

^{1}/$_2$ cup apple, diced

1. Preheat oven to 425 degrees.

2. Combine dry ingredients.

3. Cut the butter into flour mixture using two knives, until the mixture resembles coarse cornmeal.

4. While lightly tossing the butter-flour mixture with a fork, add the liquids. Stir until the dough holds together.

5. Turn dough onto a lightly floured board. Knead about 10 times.

6. Roll dough thin to ^{1}/$_4$" or a bit less, if possible. Cut into 2" rounds with a floured glass.

7. Put half of the cut biscuits on a baking sheet.

8. Combine diced pork (or chicken) and apple. Place about 1 tablespoon on each biscuit.

9. Cover with the remaining biscuits. Press edges together to seal for baking.

10. Bake for 12–15 minutes until lightly browned. Serve warm with butter.

YIELD: 10 2" biscuits

PREPARATION TIME: 30 minutes

BAKING TIME: 15 minutes

VARIATIONS: Both the fillings and the size and shape of these can be changed. Add chutney or raisins to this filling. Fill biscuits with partially cooked pork, turkey, sausage, or ham and cheese. Smaller shapes can be served as an hors d'oeuvre. Try larger 8" circles folded in half to make turnovers. To borrow the Cornish pasty idea, stuff with leftovers such as cooked meat, grated carrots, potatoes, turnips, salt, and pepper and make these turnovers into full meals. Experiment with your combinations including leftover gravy or cream.

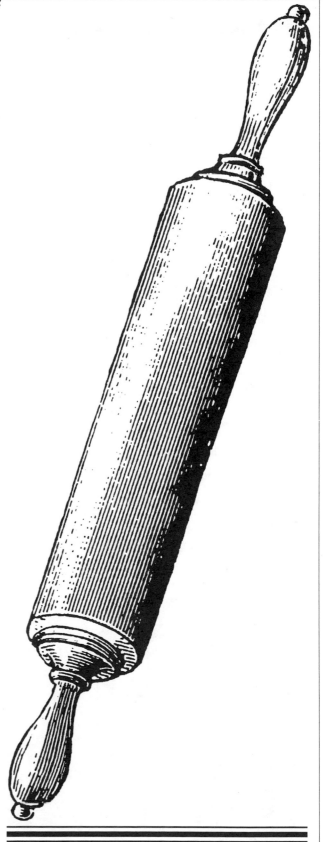

Crumbed Chicken in Wine Sauce

I made this for my first-ever dinner party. I was quite nervous and took comfort by how much could be prepared in advance. The meal turned out fine, but what I best remember was the table decoration — a wild grapevine with leaves placed along the center of the table with small votive candles dotted between the leaves. It is a favorite table setting to this day.

CHICKEN

8–10 chicken breast halves

Salt and pepper

2/3 cup plain yogurt or light sour cream

6 tablespoons butter or margarine, melted

2 cups fresh bread crumbs

SAUCE

1/2 cup dry white wine

1 onion, chopped

6 peppercorns

1 bay leaf

1 strip lemon rind

1 tablespoon mixed fresh herbs (thyme, sage, marjoram, tarragon), or 1 teaspoon dried herbs

2/3 cup plain or light sour cream

Salt

1. Rinse and pat chicken dry with a paper towel. Season with salt and pepper.

2. Arrange pieces in a single layer in a shallow dish. Spread with sour cream.

3. Cover and refrigerate 4 hours or overnight. Turn once or twice, respreading sour cream, as you turn.

4. Preheat oven to 375 degrees.

5. Combine melted butter and bread crumbs. Coat chicken well on all sides with this mixture.

6. Arrange in baking dish. Bake, covered with foil, for 15 minutes.

7. Take foil off chicken and continue to bake until browned, 15–20 minutes, turning once or twice.

8. While chicken is baking (or in advance), begin sauce. Put wine, onion, peppercorns, bay leaf, lemon rind, and herbs in a small saucepan. Cover and bring to a boil. Simmer gently for 5 minutes.

9. Uncover and continue to boil until sauce is reduced by half.

10. Strain. (After straining, sauce can be refrigerated until serving or proceed.)

11. When ready to serve, stir 2/3 cup sour cream into sauce and add salt to taste. Heat gently; do not boil. Serve sauce in gravy boat to be ladled over chicken.

YIELD: 6–8 servings

PREPARATION TIME: Under 30 minutes

MARINATING AND BAKING TIME: 5 hours or more

Hot Stuffed Italian Bread

Wrap this in foil and several layers of newspaper while the bread is still warm and the cheese still bubbly. We've taken it in the woods to eat when cutting wood, to the field during baseball games, and on walks when checking out the progress of the season.

2 tablespoons olive oil

2 cloves garlic, finely chopped

1 cup drained tomatoes

1/4 cup red or white wine

Salt and pepper

Pinch basil

1 baguette or similar long loaf of French or Italian bread

6–8 slices Genoa salami

6–8 slices provolone cheese

Red onions

Red and green peppers, optional

Black olives, optional

Freshly grated Parmesan cheese

1. Heat olive oil and garlic together. Do not let garlic brown. Add tomatoes and simmer gently for 5 minutes. Add wine, bring to a boil, and reduce sauce by half. Add seasonings.

2. Split loaf of bread lengthwise and brush with olive oil. Spread 2–3 tablespoons of sauce over each half of bread.

3. Depending on width of bread, slice salami and cheese in half, if necessary. Alternate layers of meat and cheese.

4. Sprinkle with chopped onions, peppers, and olives. Drizzle with additional olive oil and sprinkle with cheese.

5. Place 5–6 inches under broiler and heat for 4 minutes. Watch to keep from burning.

YIELD: 2–4 servings
PREPARATION TIME: 15 minutes

CREAMED CHICKEN WITH VERMONT CORN BREAD

We always had good, fresh chicken on hand. This is a plain, comforting meal.

3 tablespoons butter or margarine

¹/₄ cup onion, chopped

3 tablespoons flour

2–3 cups chicken broth (rich broth in which chicken was simmered, or canned)

4 cups chicken, cooked and cut into bite-sized pieces

Salt and pepper

1. Melt butter and saute onion until softened.

2. Remove from heat, stir in flour, and cook over low heat for 2 minutes, stirring.

3. Whisk in broth, a little at a time.

4. Cook 15 minutes over low heat.

5. Add chicken, and season with salt and pepper.

YIELD: 4 servings

PREPARATION TIME: 10 minutes

COOKING TIME: 15 minutes

VARIATION: Add pimentos, mushrooms, or peas in step 1 for a colorful and tasty alternative.

VERMONT CORN BREAD

Corn bread is such a versatile food — made either spicy or sweet. In winter, I love it as a base for Creamed Chicken or Spicy Stewed Eggplant (page 46).

1/4 cup maple syrup

1/4 cup brown sugar

2 eggs

2 cups flour

1 tablespoon baking powder

3/4 teaspoon salt

1 cup cornmeal

1 1/2 cups low-fat milk

4 tablespoons butter or margarine, melted

1. Preheat oven to 425 degrees. Grease a 13" x 9" pan.

2. Mix syrup and sugar in a bowl. Beat in eggs.

3. Sift flour, baking powder, and salt together. Stir into egg mixture.

4. Add cornmeal and beat.

5. Add milk and about half of the butter. Mix well.

6. Pour into pan, spreading evenly. Bake 25 minutes.

7. Brush with the remaining butter.

PREPARATION TIME: 5 minutes
COOKING TIME: 25 minutes

Lamb Medallions with Potato Parmesan Crust

We raised sheep on Uphill Farm, so lamb was often served at our table. This recipe wraps tender lamb in a blanket of potato and cheese, allowing the lamb to season the crust from the inside. This is a dress-up dinner entree for company.

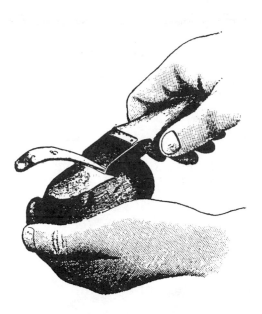

3 medium-sized potatoes (1¹/2 pounds), cooked and drained

2 shallots or 1 small white onion, finely chopped

3 garlic cloves, minced

1 teaspoon rosemary

Salt and pepper

12 1¹/2" lamb medallions (cut from approximately 24 ounces of boneless lamb loin)

¹/2 cup freshly grated Parmesan cheese

¹/4 cup olive oil

1. Grate potatoes in food processor.

2. In bowl, mix with shallots and garlic.

3. Rub rosemary, salt, and pepper into lamb.

4. Grate Parmesan onto waxed paper.

5. Press cheese into lamb to coat.

6. Divide potato mixture into 12 mounds. Surround medallions with potatoes using palms of hands.

7. Heat 2 tablespoons oil in skillet. When hot, add lamb.

8. Cook approximately 3 minutes per side, until potatoes are a crusty brown. Use tongs to turn and brown sides.

9. Lamb will keep in a 225 degree oven while you continue to cook remaining medallions.

YIELD: 4–6 servings
PREPARATION TIME: 30 minutes
COOKING TIME: 20 minutes

TORTELLINI IN A SAUSAGE CREAM SAUCE

Freshly made lean sausage is one of the great rewards of raising pigs. It's the only sausage I ever eat, and this is a quick and delicious use for it.

1 (8-ounce) package of tortellini

1/2 pound good quality lean bulk pork or turkey sausage

Olive oil, as needed

1 clove garlic, minced

1/2 teaspoon rosemary, optional

Freshly ground black pepper

1 cup half-and-half or cream

1/3 cup freshly grated Parmesan cheese (or part cheddar)

1. Cook pasta according to package directions.

2. While pasta is cooking, brown sausage in a skillet. Depending on the fat in the sausage, add oil if needed to keep sausage from sticking, or drain, if fat is excessive.

3. Stir in garlic, rosemary, and pepper. Cook a few minutes more.

4. Add cream. When mixture begins to bubble, add the cheese.

5. Put tortellini on a warm platter. Spoon on sausage sauce and serve immediately. Garnish with parsley.

YIELD: 4–6 servings

PREPARATION TIME: 15 minutes

VARIATIONS: Finely chop a small onion and add to browning sausage. For a thicker sauce, add a scant tablespoon of flour to the sausage before adding the half-and-half.

GARNISHES

It's fun to add your own style to the way you present dishes. Often it's the simplest touches that can be most effective. A small red maple leaf adds seasonal beauty to a bowl of unshelled nuts, as does an individual sprig of thyme centered on a whole pork roast.

FAVORITE GARNISHES

Garnishes are a way to add your personal touch to any meal. For days when the chores last too long or the office is too hectic, it's the little gestures that often give the most pleasure. A sprig of bittersweet at each place setting can refocus everyone to the joy of the season and of being together.

Here are some ideas that have worked well for me:

Herb wreaths

Whole sprigs of herbs

Violets

Molded herb butters

Fruit or vegetable candle-holders

Rings of daisies and red clover

Bouquets in middle of cake

Sugared rose petals and pansy petals

Chive blossoms

Day-lily blossoms

Grape vines

UPHILL FARM PIES, TARTS, & CAKES

April Lemon Cake

Sour Cream Cupcakes with Maple Frosting

Chocolate Chip Pecan Pie

Mocha Fudge Tart

Basic Pastries

Blueberry Cake with Lemon Meringue Sauce

Hillside Peach Shortcake

Renate's Swedish Cake

Betty Bacon's Frosted Layer Cake

Uphill Farm Apple Tart

Vermont Upside-Down Cake

December's Cake

Uphill Farm's Bûche de Nöel

Mrs. Wilson's Cake

Washington's Birthday Pie

April Lemon Cake

This lemony cake is for those warm April days that hold the promise of summer — when local fruit is not yet available, but we are anticipating the lighter tastes of the coming season. It is a rich cake, so thin slices are just right.

CAKE

1^1/$_2$ sticks sweet butter, softened

1^1/$_2$ cups sugar

2 eggs

1^1/$_4$ cups flour

^{1}/$_2$ teaspoon baking soda

^{1}/$_2$ teaspoon salt

^{3}/$_4$ cup buttermilk

1^1/$_2$ tablespoons lemon zest, freshly grated

1^1/$_2$ tablespoons lemon juice

FILLING

Grated zest of 2 lemons

^{1}/$_2$ cup lemon juice (about 2 lemons)

1 cup sugar

2 tablespoons water

2 eggs, beaten

2 tablespoons butter

2 tablespoons flour

ICING

4 tablespoons sweet butter

2 cups confectioners' sugar

Grated zest of 1 lemon

^{1}/$_4$ cup lemon juice

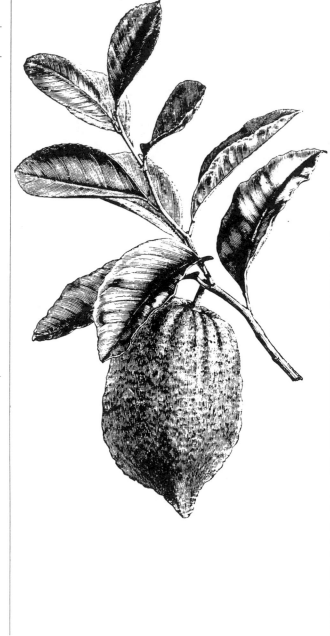

CAKE

1. Preheat oven to 325 degrees.

2. Butter a single 9" springform pan.

3. In mixer, beat butter and sugar together until fluffy and light. Then, beat in eggs, one at a time.

4. Sift together flour, soda, and salt. Add dry ingredients alternately with buttermilk. Start and end with dry ingredients.

5. Stir in lemon zest and juice.

6. Spoon into springform pan. Bake for 1 hour or until a toothpick comes out clean.

7. Cool 15 minutes and remove cake from the pan.

8. Keeping cake on the pan bottom, slice into 2 layers. Remove top layer.

FILLING

1. In a heavy-bottomed pan, combine filling ingredients and stir continuously over medium-low heat until thickened.

2. Strain filling into bowl. Let cool slightly.

3. Pour warm filling onto cooled cake and spread. Put top layer over filling.

ICING

1. Cream butter and sugar in mixer.

2. Add zest and juice.

3. Beat until smooth and spreadable. Then, ice the top and sides of cake.

YIELD: 10–12 servings
PREPARATION TIME: 1¹/₂ hours

SOUR CREAM CUPCAKES WITH MAPLE FROSTING

These are delicate little cakes — and not too sweet. I remember Owen reading aloud one evening by candlelight after we'd lost our power during a storm. Abby and Clem were little, snuggled together in a brown, velvety chair. We had tea with these cakes and watched the lightening down the valley.

CUPCAKES

1/2 cup butter

3/4 cup granulated sugar

2 eggs

1 cup sour cream

1/2 teaspoon baking soda

1 tablespoon hot water

1 1/3 cups flour

1/4 teaspoon salt

1 teaspoon baking powder

1 tablespoon vanilla extract

FROSTING

2 tablespoons butter

2 cups confectioners' sugar

1/4 teaspoon salt

4 tablespoons pure maple syrup

1. Preheat oven to 375 degrees.

2. To prepare cupcakes, cream butter. Gradually add sugar, creaming until light.

3. Mix in eggs, beating well after each addition. Add sour cream; stir well.

4. Dissolve baking soda in water. Mix in.

5. Sift flour with salt and baking powder. Gradually fold sifted ingredients into the butter mixture. Add the vanilla.

6. Grease and lightly flour cupcake tins. Fill to 2/3-full.

7. Bake for 15–20 minutes. Cool on racks.

8. To prepare frosting, cream butter. Sift confectioners' sugar and gradually add with salt to butter.

9. Stir in syrup; then beat until smooth and spreadable. Frost well-cooled cupcakes.

YIELD: 12 cupcakes

PREPARATION TIME: 30 minutes

BAKING TIME: 20 minutes

CHOCOLATE CHIP PECAN PIE

When my son Slater was 10 years old, he won second place in a July 4th pie-baking contest with this recipe. The rich chocolate-pecan filling is best when served with unsweetened whipped cream.

1 9" pie crust, unbaked (see page 114)

3 eggs

1¼ cups granulated sugar

½ cup flour

5 tablespoons sweet butter, melted

1¼ cups semisweet chocolate bits

1½ cups chopped pecans

½ teaspoon salt

½ teaspoon vanilla extract

½ cup light corn syrup

1. Preheat oven to 350 degrees.

2. Beat eggs well in a bowl.

3. Stir in remaining ingredients.

4. Pour into pastry shell. Bake for 45 minutes.

YIELD: 10 servings
PREPARATION TIME: 15 minutes
BAKING TIME: 45 minutes

Mocha Fudge Tart

This unbaked tart was an Uphill Farm favorite. It's very easy to prepare, but start it early in the day as it requires several hours of refrigeration.

CRUST

1$\frac{1}{3}$ cups chocolate wafer cookie crumbs

6 tablespoons unsalted butter, melted

FILLING

1 cup granulated sugar

2 tablespoons flour

$\frac{1}{8}$ teaspoon salt

$\frac{1}{4}$ cup light cream

2 eggs, at room temperature

1 tablespoon instant coffee powder

1 cup boiling water

2 ounces unsweetened chocolate

4 tablespoons unsalted butter

1 teaspoon vanilla extract

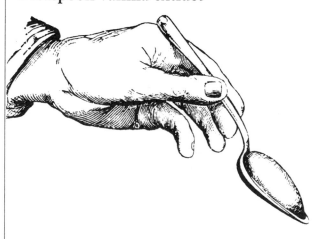

TOPPING

$\frac{2}{3}$ cup whipping cream

1 tablespoon confectioners' sugar

$\frac{1}{2}$ teaspoon vanilla extract

Semisweet chocolate for grating

1. Lightly grease an 8" springform pan.

2. Combine cookie crumbs and 6 tablespoons melted butter. Press crust on the bottom and about 2 inches up the sides of the pan.

3. Refrigerate crust for at least 30 minutes.

4. Meanwhile, prepare filling in a heavy-bottomed saucepan. Mix the sugar, flour, and salt in the saucepan. Stir in the cream and eggs.

5. Mix the coffee in the boiling water. Place the saucepan over low heat. Gradually pour in the boiling coffee, stirring constantly.

6. Continue stirring until filling comes to a boil. Stir and boil for 1 minute.

7. Remove from heat. Stir in the chocolate and the butter. Set the pan in a bowl, partially filled with ice water. Beat the mixture.

8. When it cools somewhat, add vanilla. Continue beating until thick, glossy, and lukewarm.

9. Spoon filling into the crumb crust, and refrigerate for about 4 hours or until firm.

10. To prepare the topping, beat the cream with the sugar and vanilla until soft peaks form.

11. Either mound the cream on top of the tart, or serve it in a bowl, spooning some alongside each slice when serving. Grate chocolate on top of cream.

YIELD: 8–10 servings
PREPARATION TIME: 30 minutes
REFRIGERATION TIME: 4 hours

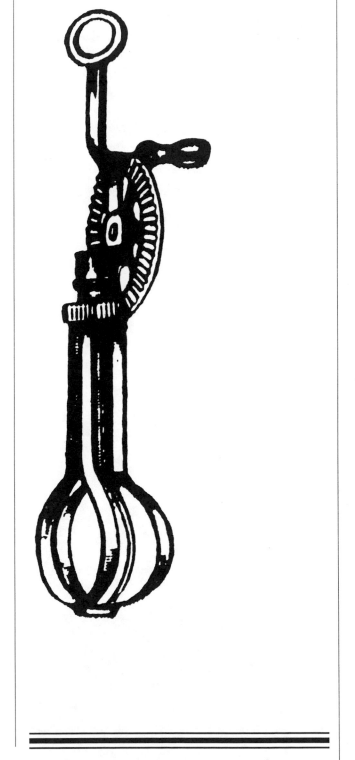

BASIC PASTRIES

There are many versions of "short crusts" with variations in the fat used being the primary difference. Traditional cooks wouldn't think of using anything but lard. I never could, and, loving the flavor butter imparts, use butter cutting it with shortening or margarine. The resulting pastry is certainly lighter than an all-butter crust, yet it's as delicious as only butter can make it.

As with all pastry, keep both the shortening and the water cold. Light handling keeps the pastry from being warmed by your hands.

I. BASIC PIE CRUST

2 cups flour

1/2 teaspoon salt

1/3 cup chilled, unsalted butter

1/3 cup vegetable shortening or margarine

4 tablespoons ice water

1. Combine flour and salt.

2. With 2 knives, cut in butter and shortening until mixture resembles coarse meal.

3. While tossing the pastry with a fork, sprinkle it with ice water, a bit at a time. Continue tossing to moisten evenly.

4. Form pastry quickly into two pieces and chill for 1/2 hour before rolling out.

5. Continue according to the recipe of your choice.

YIELD: 2 9" crusts or 1 double crust

PREPARATION TIME: 10 minutes

VARIATION: For whole wheat pastry, use whatever proportion whole wheat flour to white flour you prefer, up to the total 2 cups flour called for. Be sure to sift the whole wheat flour to separate out any bran, husk, or solids. Reserve these solids to enrich other foods.

II. SOUR CREAM PASTRY

1½ cups unbleached white flour

2 sticks butter, chilled

½ cup sour cream

1. Using two knives or a pastry blender, cut the butter into the flour. The resulting mixture will look like coarse crumbs.

2. Stir in sour cream.

3. In a bowl, lightly knead pastry until it just holds its shape.

4. Wrap in plastic wrap and refrigerate a few hours or overnight.

5. Continue on with recipe of your choice.

YIELD: 1 pie crust

PREPARATION TIME: 10 minutes

REFRIGERATION TIME: 3 hours or overnight

BLUEBERRY CAKE WITH LEMON MERINGUE SAUCE

My mother is a tireless blueberry picker, so each year I've made this moist cake for her and her efforts. It's a first rate reward after a day of picking.

The cake can be prepared ahead, but save the sauce for the last minute.

2 cups fresh blueberries

1/4 cup butter

1/2 cup granulated sugar

1 egg

1 teaspoon vanilla extract

1 3/4 cups flour

1 1/2 teaspoons baking powder

1/2 teaspoon salt

1/3 cup milk

1/4 teaspoon cinnamon

TOPPING

4 tablespoons butter

1/2 cup granulated sugar

1/2 cup flour

1. Preheat oven to 375 degrees.

2. Wash and drain blueberries in a sieve.

3. Cream 1/4 cup butter and 1/2 cup sugar until light; beat in egg and vanilla.

4. In a smaller mixing bowl, combine flour, baking powder, and salt.

5. Beginning and ending with the dry ingredients, alternately add flour mixture and milk to the creamed butter. Mix to just blend.

6. Spoon batter into a greased 9" round cake pan. Smooth top.

7. Gently dry blueberries with a towel, and spread over the batter. Sprinkle with cinnamon.

8. To prepare topping, combine butter, sugar, and flour with fingers until crumbly. Sprinkle topping over berries.

9. Bake for 45 minutes.

10. Remove cake from oven and cool slightly on rack. Serve warm with Lemon Meringue Sauce.

YIELD: 8 servings
PREPARATION TIME: 20 minutes
BAKING TIME: 45 minutes

LEMON MERINGUE SAUCE

Sometimes I substitute dried lemon peel, although there is nothing like the flavor of fresh lemons. For zest, use only the thin yellow layer of rind; the white inner layer is bitter. A small tool, with four or five small holes, called a zester, is very handy and does a good job.

This sauce is excellent served over fresh berries, winter fruit salads, frozen desserts, and cakes.

3 egg yolks

3/4 cup granulated sugar

1/4 cup lemon juice

1 teaspoon grated lemon zest

2 egg whites

1. Beat yolks until very light and thick.

2. Add half of the sugar (6 tablespoons) and continue beating until well mixed.

3. Stir in lemon juice and zest.

4. Transfer mixture to the top of a double boiler. Stir it over simmering water until sauce is thick and smooth, about 5 minutes.

5. Beat whites of 2 eggs. When they begin to foam, add remaining 6 tablespoons sugar and continue beating until soft peaks form.

6. Fold whites into lemon-yolk sauce thoroughly.

7. Serve in a crystal bowl, and ladle onto cake slices.

YIELD: 2 cups

PREPARATION TIME: 25 minutes

HILLSIDE PEACH SHORTCAKE

Running parallel to the farmhouse porch was a stone wall, and alongside it were fragrant hydrangea, roses, iris, and flowering raspberry bushes. Evenings, we'd sit on the porch, enjoy the sweet night air, and, sometimes, this sweet peach shortcake.

5 tablespoons butter or margarine

1 cup flour

2/3 cup sugar

2 teaspoons baking powder

1/4 teaspoon salt

1 egg, slightly beaten

2 tablespoons milk

Sugar

4 cups unpeeled peaches, sliced

2 tablespoons lemon juice,
or 1 teaspoon almond extract

Whipping cream

Confectioners' sugar

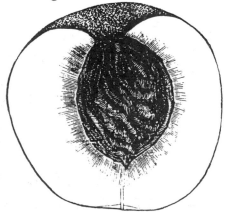

1. Preheat the oven to 400 degrees.

2. Separate 2 tablespoons butter, and set aside.

3. Mix flour, 2 tablespoons sugar, baking powder, and salt.

4. Cut in 3 tablespoons of the butter until it resembles coarse meal.

5. Add egg and milk. Toss to form soft dough. Knead gently on lightly floured surface. Roll to 1/4" thickness and cut into 12 2 1/2" rounds.

6. Place 6 rounds on a cookie tray. Spread each with a bit of butter. Top with the remaining rounds. Sprinkle tops with sugar.

7. Bake for about 15 minutes or until golden.

8. Toss peaches with sugar and juice. Let sit. Allow shortcakes to cool slightly. Separate in half.

9. Beat cream with sugar to taste.

10. Spoon peaches over bottom half. Then spoon some cream over peaches, and cover with top cake. Spoon more cream over peach-filled shortcakes.

YIELD: 6 servings

PREPARATION TIME: 40 minutes

VARIATION: Raspberries are delicious when combined with peaches. Try them together.

RENATE'S SWEDISH CAKE

A quickly prepared, buttery cake that our friend Renate introduced to Uphill Farm. Carry it in the pan to a picnic, or serve it with iced tea on the porch. The top is macaroon-like and needs no additional topping.

3 eggs

1½ cups granulated sugar

1½ sticks butter, melted

1½ cups flour

Optional flavorings to taste:

> Orange peel
>
> Cardamon
>
> Nutmeg
>
> Nuts

1. Preheat oven to 350 degrees.

2. Beat 3 eggs with the sugar.

3. Add melted butter, flour, and optional flavorings.

4. Pour batter into a single 9" round cake pan.

5. Bake for 40 minutes. Check cake. When it is a light brown, turn off oven and let cake cool in oven.

6. To serve, cut in thin wedges.

PREPARATION TIME: 15 minutes
BAKING TIME: 40 minutes

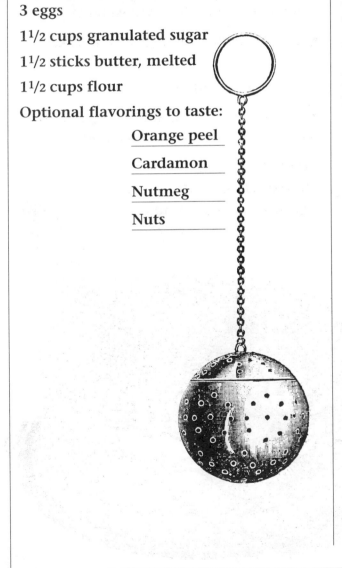

BETTY BACON'S FROSTED LAYER CAKE

An all-time favorite yellow cake with a dark and buttery chocolate icing. Betty Bacon was the best cook I knew when I was a child, and a true inspiration to me. I remember making all sorts of excuses to visit her after school to watch her cook, hoping for a cake and milk invitation. It's been many years since I've seen her, but this cake remains the ultimate comforting cake, and my family's favorite birthday cake.

For better cakes, always have all cake ingredients as close to room temperature as possible. When preparing cake batters, the butter and sugar should be well creamed and the eggs well beaten. After the eggs are beaten, gently mix or fold in the remaining dry and liquid ingredients with a rubber spatula or wooden spoon. When adding wet and dry ingredients to the batter alternately, begin and end with the dry ingredients.

1. Preheat the oven to 375 degrees.

2. Cream the butter. Gradually add the sugar, while continuing to cream until light and fluffy.

3. Add eggs, one at a time, beating well after each addition.

4. Sift dry ingredients together.

5. Alternately, blend the dry ingredients and the milk into the creamed butter.

6. Divide batter into 2 greased 8" cake pans.

7. Bake for 25 minutes.

8. Cool on a rack for 5 minutes, and turn out of pans. When completely cool, frost.

YIELD: 12 servings
PREPARATION TIME: 30 minutes
BAKING TIME: 25 minutes

1/2 cup butter, at room temperature

1 1/2 cups granulated sugar

3 eggs

2 cups flour

2 teaspoons baking powder

Pinch salt

1 cup milk

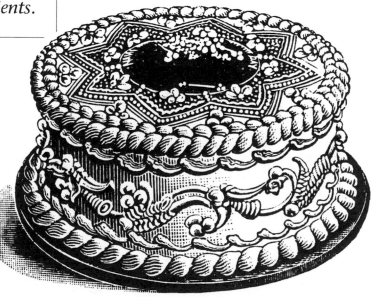

FAVORITE CHOCOLATE ICING

4 squares unsweetened chocolate

2 1/2 cups confectioners' sugar

1 teaspoon vanilla extract

1/4 cup water

1 egg

6 tablespoons butter, melted

1. Melt chocolate in the top of a double boiler.

2. Remove saucepan from hot water. Add sugar, vanilla, and water, beating until stiff.

3. Add egg and butter, mixing until smooth and spreadable.

4. Allow icing to set for a while, if it needs to thicken.

5. For ease in frosting, dip knife in hot water. Apply icing to the sides of the cake first, then frost the top. After joining top and sides, smooth sides with one final, even stroke.

YIELD: Frosting for top, middle, and sides of layer cake.

PREPARATION TIME: 5 minutes

UPHILL FARM APPLE TART

We picked bushels of apples every year. I used them in a lot of my cooking, and this became one of my favorite apple desserts. Spoon calvados-flavored whipped cream alongside each serving.

1 cup plus 2 tablespoons unbleached flour

1/2 teaspoon salt

1 teaspoon granulated sugar

1 teaspoon baking powder

1/2 cup butter or margarine

1 egg yolk

2 tablespoons calvados, brandy, or rum

4 apples, peeled, cored, and cut in eighths

2 tablespoons sliced almonds

TOPPING

1/2 – 2/3 cup granulated sugar

2 tablespoons flour

1/2 teaspoon ground cinnamon

2 tablespoons butter, softened

1. Preheat oven to 350 degrees.

2. Combine dry ingredients.

3. Cut in butter, using 2 knives.

4. Add the egg yolk and calvados. Combine with fingers.

5. Press dough into a 9" pan, bringing up sides to form an edge.

6. Arrange sliced apples in concentric circles or other pattern. Sprinkle with almonds.

7. Make a topping, combining sugar, flour, cinnamon, and butter. Sprinkle over apples and almonds.

8. Bake for 45 minutes.

9. Remove to rack to cool.

YIELD: 8 servings
PREPARATION TIME: 30 minutes
BAKING TIME: 45 minutes

Vermont Upside-Down Cake

What better way to celebrate autumn than with freshly picked apples and Vermont maple syrup! Turn this cake out of its pan and a flowery pattern of apples appears. A lovely cake for an outdoor brunch, as it isn't too sweet.

TOPPING

3 tablespoons butter

1/2 cup pure maple syrup

2 tablespoons sliced almonds

2 apples (macintosh), washed and cored, not peeled

CAKE

4 tablespoons butter

1/3 cup granulated sugar

1/2 teaspoon vanilla extract

2 eggs

1 1/2 cups flour

1/4 teaspoon salt

2 teaspoons baking powder

1/2 cup milk

Whipped cream

1. Preheat oven to 350 degrees.

2. In an 8" or 9" skillet (or 9" cake pan), melt 3 tablespoons butter. Pour in maple syrup and sprinkle on almonds.

3. Slice apples in 1/2" rings. Then, cut all the rings in half except one.

4. Place the single whole apple ring in the center of the buttery pan. Arrange the remaining slices in a ring around the central one. Set aside.

5. To prepare the batter, cream the 4 tablespoons butter with the sugar until light and fluffy. Beat in the vanilla. Add the eggs, one at a time, beating well after each addition.

6. Sift together the flour, salt, and baking powder. Add this to the creamed mixture in 3 parts, alternating with the milk. Combine well.

7. Pour the batter over the apples and bake for 45 minutes.

8. Remove from oven and cool in the pan for 5 minutes on a rack.

9. While still warm, turn upside down on a serving dish. Serve warm and pass whipped cream separately.

YIELD: 8 servings
PREPARATION TIME: 15 minutes
BAKING TIME: 45 minutes

DECEMBER'S CAKE
A Walnut Pound Cake

I make and freeze many of these cakes early in December, defrost them, and then glaze them as needed for holiday giving. One year, Elly and Sarah stuck a small toy tow truck on top. It was a present for their mechanic, a local hero who helped get their old cars through the Vermont winter.

1¹/2 cups sifted flour

1/4 teaspoon baking soda

1¹/4 cups granulated sugar

1 cup butter, room temperature

1¹/2 tablespoons lemon juice

¹/2 teaspoon almond extract

5 eggs, separated

1 cup coarsely chopped walnuts or pecans

¹/8 teaspoon salt

1 teaspoon cream of tartar

GLAZE

1 cup sifted confectioners' sugar

¹/2 teaspoon vanilla extract

1 teaspoon milk

1. Preheat oven to 325 degrees.

2. Butter and flour a 9" tube pan.

3. Mix flour, baking soda, and ³/4 cup granulated sugar into a bowl.

4. Add butter, and blend in with your fingers or a wooden spoon.

5. Add lemon juice and extract. Mix in egg yolks one at a time, blending well after each addition.

6. Fold in coarsely chopped nuts.

7. In a separate bowl, beat egg whites until stiff. Gradually add remaining granulated sugar, cream of tartar, and salt to the stiff egg whites.

8. Fold egg whites into the nut batter until thoroughly incorporated.

9. Spoon into pan and spread evenly.

10. Bake for about 1 hour. Turn off heat and let cake remain in oven for an additional 10–15 minutes.

11. Invert on rack covered with waxed paper to cool.

12. When cool, wrap well to freeze, or make the following glaze to use if serving immediately.

13. Add vanilla and milk to the sifted confectioners' sugar. Amounts are approximate and should be adjusted to make the glaze easy to spread.

YIELD: 10 servings
PREPARATION TIME: 30 minutes
BAKING TIME: 70 minutes

UPHILL FARM'S BÛCHE DE NÖEL

A Chocolate Roll with a Chestnut Cream Filling

On the sideboard, set apart from all the tinsel and glitter of Christmas, we have our yule log, surrounded by fir boughs. As the lights and excitement of the day dim, after the spirited dinner has been shared, we gather, quietly, each reflecting on the specialness, the affections, and generosities of the day.

And, in the candles' last glow, we share the yule log — a symbol of the extraordinary disguised in the ordinary.

CHOCOLATE ROLL

4 eggs, separated

3 tablespoons cocoa

1/4 cup flour

3/4 cup granulated sugar

1/2 teaspoon vanilla extract

  Pinch salt

FILLING

1 3/4 cups whipping cream

1/2 cup sweetened chestnut puree

2 tablespoons rum

2 tablespoons confectioners' sugar (or less to taste)

ICING

3/4 cup semisweet chocolate pieces

3 tablespoons unsalted butter

1 tablespoon cream

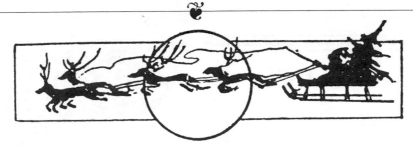

1. Preheat oven to 325 degrees. Grease a 10½" x 15½" x 1" jelly roll pan. Line with waxed paper that overhangs the pan's edges. Grease and flour the waxed paper.

2. Mix together flour and cocoa. Set aside.

3. Beat egg yolks for 4–5 minutes, until thick. Gradually add half the sugar (6 tablespoons) and continue beating. Add vanilla and beat 4 more minutes, until thick.

4. Gently fold cocoa and flour mixture into the yolks.

5. Add a pinch of salt to egg whites in a separate bowl. With clean beaters, beat until foamy. Gradually add the remaining sugar and beat at high speed, until stiff and glossy.

6. With the rubber spatula, fold ¼ of the egg whites into the chocolate-yolk mixture.

7. Then, carefully fold the chocolate mixture into the remaining egg whites.

8. Pour the batter into the prepared pan; smooth evenly. Bake 20 minutes or until top springs back when lightly touched.

9. Turn cake out onto a slightly damp dish towel. Peel off waxed paper. Trim any hard edges. Roll up, starting from a long side with the towel. Let rolled cake cool on a rack.

10. To prepare cream filling: Whip cream until soft peaks form. Beat in chestnut puree, rum, and sugar to taste. Continue beating until stiff peaks form.

11. Carefully unroll the cake. Spread with the chestnut cream. Reroll the cake, using the towel to help lift it. Slide it, seam side down onto a wooden platter, long basket, or serving dish.

12. To prepare frosting: In top of a double boiler, over hot but not boiling water, melt chocolate and butter with the cream. Stir until smooth. Let set for a few minutes.

13. Quickly spread the frosting over the roll. Run the tines of a fork along the roll to resemble bark.

14. Adorn as you wish, perhaps with a dusting of confectioners' sugar to resemble snow.

15. To serve, slice with a serrated knife in a sawing motion so as not to crush the log.

PREPARATION TIME: 50 minutes
BAKING TIME: 20 minutes

MRS. WILSON'S CAKE

Mrs. Wilson's Cake can be made in about the time it takes to do the supper dishes.

A mixing bowl and an 8"-square pan are all you need. Or if you wish, double this recipe and bake in an 11" x 7" pan. The topping here is chewy and sweet; some may prefer this without its icing.

CAKE

1 cup granulated sugar

1 1/2 cups flour

3 tablespoons cocoa

1/2 teaspoon salt

1 teaspoon baking soda

5 tablespoons butter, melted

1 tablespoon cider vinegar

1 teaspoon vanilla extract

1 cup cold water

TOPPING

1/2 cup packed brown sugar

3 tablespoons butter, melted

3 tablespoons light cream

1. Preheat oven to 400 degrees.

2. Sift sugar, flour, cocoa, salt, and baking soda into a bowl.

3. Make a well in the center, and add melted butter and the liquid ingredients. Beat well.

4. Pour into an 8" square pan. Bake for 30 minutes. Cool completely before spreading topping.

5. For topping, mix together brown sugar, butter, and light cream.

6. Spread over the cooled cake and set under broiler for 1 minute. Watch carefully to prevent burning.

7. Allow frosting to cool. Serve from pan.

YIELD: 12–16 pieces
PREPARATION TIME: 15 minutes
BAKING TIME: 30 minutes

WASHINGTON'S BIRTHDAY PIE

Most years our children act out their own version of "Little George's" cherry tree incident. And every year we end the play with applause and this pie. The first year, our shy little George never quite got past chopping the tree down, repeatedly knocking it over and setting it back up again. Despite his single-minded performance, he did understand the point. During dessert, he looked up and said, in all candor, "Mom. I can not tell a lie; I hate this cherry pie."
   Some of us love it!

1$\frac{1}{3}$ cups granulated sugar

4 tablespoons flour

$\frac{1}{8}$ teaspoon salt

$\frac{1}{4}$ teaspoon almond extract

$\frac{1}{3}$ cup water (or liquid from drained canned cherries)

1$\frac{1}{2}$ pounds (4 cups) fresh, pitted, sour red cherries or 3 cups canned water-packed sour red cherries, drained and liquid reserved

1 9" double pastry crust, unbaked (see page 114)

2 tablespoons butter

Milk and sugar, optional

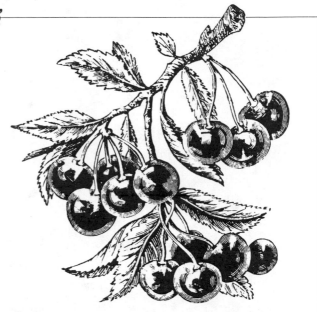

1. Preheat oven to 425 degrees.

2. Combine sugar, flour, salt, extract, liquid, and mix with the cherries.

3. Roll out pastry. Place half in a 9" pie tin.

4. Pour in cherry mixture. Dot with butter. Cut and trim bottom crust to have about a 1" overhang.

5. Roll remaining half pastry and cut into $\frac{1}{2}$" strips. Weave strips in a lattice over pie. Seal edges.

6. The lattice can be brushed with milk and sprinkled with sugar.

7. Bake for 10 minutes; reduce heat to 350 degrees and continue baking for 30 minutes more.

Tip: This is a bubbly pie. Put a baking sheet on a lower oven shelf to catch spills.

YIELD: 8 servings

PREPARATION TIME: 30 minutes

BAKING TIME: 40 minutes

VARIATION: 3 tablespoons of tapioca or 3 tablespoons cornstarch can substitute for 4 tablespoons flour.

FAVORITE COUNTRY DESSERTS

Rhubarb Trifle

Maple Floating Islands

Raspberries in Crème Anglaise

Uphill Farm Iced Brownies

Pears in Crème Caramel

Compote of Summer Berries

Poached Apricots with Almond Whipped Cream

Hot Fudge Sauce

Strawberries with Lemon Cream

Country Baked Apples

Pumpkin Bread Pudding with Whiskey Hard Sauce

Mother's Rice Pudding

Wild Farm Maple Cottage Pudding

Toblerone™ Fondue

Holiday Florentines

Frosted Brown Cow Cookies

Rhubarb Trifle

Rhubarb is the first spring fruit to ripen in Vermont. Most old farms have rhubarb plants. During the season we'd have stewed rhubarb and rhubarb cobblers and crisps. This recipe is for special occasions. Trifles are not hard to make, but they do take some time. Separate it into its three component parts: cake layers, fruit layers, and crème anglaise. Each can be made separately and in advance. The completed trifle needs at least 6 hours of refrigeration before serving. Trifle should be assembled in a deep, straight-sided glass bowl.

The recipe for Crème Anglaise is basic. The only trick in preparation is to keep the heat low — when heat is too high, the egg yolks will curdle.

1. Preheat oven to 325 degrees. Grease an 8" springform pan.

2. Beat the egg yolks. Gradually add sugar and continue beating until light and fluffy. Stir in flavoring.

3. Gently fold flour into the yolk mixture.

4. In a separate bowl, beat egg whites and salt until just stiff. Fold 1/4 of white into the yolk-flour mixture to lighten it. Then fold in remaining whites.

5. Pour into the greased pan. Bake 45 minutes.

6. Let cool on wire rack. Wrap in plastic wrap until time to assemble.

7. When ready to assemble, split the cake into 4 thin layers, using a long, sharp knife and a sawing motion.

CAKE LAYERS

6 eggs, separated

2/3–3/4 cup granulated sugar

1/2 teaspoon vanilla or lemon extract

1 1/2 cups minus 2 tablespoons flour

Pinch salt

Sherry for brushing on layers

FRUIT LAYER

5–6 cups rhubarb, cut in 2" lengths

3/4 cup granulated sugar

1/2 cup water

1. Combine rhubarb, sugar, and water in a heavy-bottomed saucepan.

2. Bring to a boil; cover and simmer for 10 minutes.

3. Uncover and stir over moderate heat until most of the liquid is gone, about 10 minutes.

4. Let cool.

CRÈME ANGLAISE

6 egg yolks

1/3 cup sugar

1/8 teaspoon salt

2 cups half-and-half or milk, scalded

1 1/2 teaspoons vanilla extract

1 tablespoon Grand Marnier, Cointreau, or sherry

6 tablespoons strawberry-rhubarb jam

1. Beat egg yolks, sugar, and salt in a heavy saucepan until light and fluffy.

2. Continue stirring, and gradually add scalded milk to the yolk mixture.

3. Cook over medium-low heat, stirring with a wooden spoon for about 10 minutes. The mixture will coat the back of a metal spoon when done. Do not boil!

4. Let cool a bit; then add vanilla and liqueur.

5. Stir occasionally to prevent film from forming.

6. Serve warm or cover and chill.

ASSEMBLY:

1. Sprinkle cut side of cake layers with sherry and spread each layer with 2 tablespoons preserves.

2. Build trifle in a deep serving dish about 8 inches in diameter. A glass dish is preferable. Spread first cake layer with 1/3 of the rhubarb and 1/2 cup of *Crème Anglaise*. Continue layering cake, fruit, and custard sauce, ending with a cake layer. Pour remaining *Crème Anglaise* over top.

3. Refrigerate for at least 6 hours.

YIELD: 8–10 servings

PREPARATION TIME: 1–1 1/2 hours (can be done in stages)

REFRIGERATION TIME: 6-plus hours

VARIATION: Variations are part of the fun of trifles. Many recipes call for ready-made sponge or pound cake, or lady fingers. These, of course, can be substituted for time-saving reasons, but they will sacrifice in taste, too. The cake layers can be doused with sherry, Kirsch, rum, or liqueurs for added flavor. Various jams can be used or can be omitted altogether. I prefer strawberry-rhubarb with this recipe, but try ginger preserves for more of a bite.

MAPLE FLOATING ISLANDS

I'd make this dessert during sugaring season. It's as lovely looking as it sounds — white puffs floating on a sea of maple custard. It is my version of "Ile Flottante," a good example of adapting a classic recipe to local ingredients on hand.

ISLANDS

3 egg whites

Pinch salt

6 tablespoons granulated sugar

CUSTARD

2 cups milk (or ¹/2 light cream, ¹/2 milk)

6 egg yolks

4 tablespoons Vermont maple syrup

1 teaspoon vanilla extract

1. Begin by preparing the islands. Beat egg whites with salt until foamy. Gradually add sugar, beating until stiff.

2. Scald the milk in a shallow pan. Drop tablespoons of the island meringues onto the milk. Poach gently for about 2 minutes on each side. Remove them with a slotted spoon and drain on a towel.

3. In a heavy-bottomed saucepan, beat the egg yolks slightly. Add the maple syrup.

4. Slowly stir in the scalded milk. Cook over very low heat, stirring constantly, until the mixture begins to thicken and coats the back of a spoon. This will take between 5 and 10 minutes. Do not allow custard to boil. Cool and stir in vanilla.

5. Pour the custard in a shallow serving dish. Float the meringue islands on top. Chill until serving.

YIELD: 4–5 servings
PREPARATION TIME: 30 minutes
COOKING TIME: 15 minutes

RASPBERRIES IN CRÈME ANGLAISE

Years ago, Owen and Slater and Davy made this as part of a Mother's Day brunch. What a great combination they discovered — wine glasses layered with the berries and thick custard sauce. It was beautiful as well as delicious.

Raspberries, divided among serving dishes

Crème Anglaise

3 cups Crème Anglaise (see page 133)

1. Prepare according to recipe on page 133.

2. Cover and chill for at least an hour, until serving berries.

3. To serve with raspberries: spoon 1/4 cup of cooled sauce over berries in individual serving glasses or bowls.

YIELD: Approximately 3 cups
PREPARATION TIME: 15–20 minutes
COOKING TIME: 10 minutes
VARIATION: Variations are infinite. This sauce is delicious over all fruits and berries, and many cakes.

UPHILL FARM ICED BROWNIES

Often after the busyness of summer days, we'd relax and play badminton in the cooler air. Sometimes these games would turn into week-long tournaments as regular players would appear. Just as regularly there would be spectators and dessert. These dense, chocolatey brownies were a favorite.

BROWNIE

$^1/_2$ cup butter, melted and cooled

1 cup sugar

1 teaspoon vanilla

2 eggs

$^1/_2$ cup flour

$^1/_2$ teaspoon baking powder

$^1/_3$ cup cocoa

$^1/_2$ teaspoon salt

$^1/_2$ cup chocolate chips

ICING

$2^1/_2$ tablespoons butter, room temperature

1 cup confectioners' sugar

$2^1/_2$ tablespoons cocoa

1 tablespoon milk

$^3/_4$ teaspoon vanilla

1. Preheat oven to 350 degrees.

2. Beat butter, sugar, and vanilla with a wooden spoon.

3. Add eggs and stir gently. Do not beat.

4. Mix together flour, baking powder, cocoa, and salt in a separate bowl.

5. Fold dry ingredients into the egg-butter mixture.

6. Fold in the chocolate chips.

7. Spoon into a 9" x 9" or 7" x 11" pan.

8. Bake for 30 minutes. Cool in pan.

9. Cream together icing ingredients. Spread on cooled brownies.

YIELD: 16 brownies
PREPARATION TIME: 15 minutes
COOKING TIME: 30 minutes

PEARS IN CRÈME CARAMEL

Beyond the kitchen porch grew a Seckel pear tree. I would pick and peel the pears, canning them whole with stems still intact. Here is a good, simple, and comforting dessert that takes advantage of pears' natural, juicy sweetness.

We would often make this for the children on Saturday nights when we left them early with a sitter. Their dinners on those nights were very simple, soft-boiled egg-and-toast sort of meals, and this dessert made the meal somewhat special, or so I imagined.

4 pears, peeled, cut in half (lengthwise) and cored

4 tablespoons granulated sugar

1–2 tablespoons butter, preferably unsalted

2/3 cup light cream

1/2 teaspoon vanilla extract

1. Preheat oven to 475 degrees.

2. Arrange pears, cut side down in a shallow buttered baking dish. They need to fit closely without much excess space.

3. Sprinkle pears with sugar. Dot with butter.

4. Bake 12 minutes, basting 2 or 3 times.

5. Mix cream and vanilla. Pour over all.

6. Stir and bake a few minutes more. Sugar will be nicely browned.

YIELD: 4–8 servings
PREPARATION TIME: 10 minutes
BAKING TIME: 15 minutes

COMPOTE OF SUMMER BERRIES

Even in Vermont summer brings occasional steamy nights. No one feels much like eating, let alone cooking. This was a cure for those waning appetites. A bonus is that it's low in fat and calories, yet still seems indulgent. Serve with frozen yogurt.

1/4 cup water

1/2 cup sugar

1 tablespoon fresh lemon juice

3 cups mixed berries and other fruit (strawberries, blueberries, raspberries, blackberries, peaches, plums, cherries), cut in small pieces

4 tablespoons sweet butter

1. Heat water and sugar; stir until sugar dissolves.

2. Add juice with fruit and cook 2–3 minutes. Juice should cover the fruit.

3. Add butter; heat until melted.

4. Spoon warm fruit into individual glass bowls. Serve alone or topped with small scoops of vanilla frozen yogurt.

YIELD: 6 servings

PREPARATION TIME: 5 minutes

VARIATION: Raspberry, strawberry, or lemon sherbets also make delicious toppings.

POACHED APRICOTS WITH ALMOND WHIPPED CREAM

I had been operating under an unspoken "apricot" rule. In Vermont, fresh apricots are only available for a very short season, and, therefore, should be enjoyed to their utmost — just as they are, eaten in hand. Cooking was for dried and canned apricots or preserves. Well . . . so goes rules. I think this dessert pays due respect to apricots . . . and then some.

Serve on clear glass dishes, garnished perhaps with a green leaf. It can all be prepared in advance, except for the whipped cream, which is always better done just prior to serving.

4–6 ripe apricots

1/2 cup granulated sugar

1 cup water

Few drops lemon juice

1/2 teaspoon lemon peel

TOPPING

3/4 cup whipping cream

2–3 tablespoons confectioners' sugar

1/2 teaspoon almond extract

1. To peel apricots, drop into boiling water for one minute. Remove and set in cold water. Skins will slip off easily.

2. Combine sugar, water, and lemon juice in a medium saucepan to make a poaching syrup. Boil syrup for 4 minutes.

3. Add apricots; reduce heat and simmer 5–7 minutes, until tender.

4. Remove apricots and chill in refrigerator. If you wish, halve apricots and remove pits. (I prefer to serve them whole.)

5. Reduce syrup to half, by boiling. Cool.

6. Whip the cream until frothy. Add sugar and extract. Continue whipping until cream is thickened but not stiff.

7. Put a spoonful of the reduced syrup in the bottom of pretty individual bowls or dessert plates. Place an apricot (or 2) on the syrup and top with a small amount of whipped cream (don't cover all of the apricot).

YIELD: 4–6 servings (or 2–3 using 2 apricots per person)

PREPARATION TIME: Under 30 minutes

COOKING TIME: 8 minutes

VARIATION: Sprinkle amaretti cookie crumbs on the apricots before spooning on whipped cream.

HOT FUDGE SAUCE

For the kid in us all, here's a delicious chocolate sauce that hardens when drizzled over your favorite ice cream. It makes a great sundae in an old and familiar way.

2 ounces unsweetened chocolate

5 tablespoons coffee

1/2 cup sugar, preferably super fine

3 tablespoons butter

1/2 teaspoon vanilla

2 teaspoons liqueur (kahlua, brandy, or rum), optional

1. Cook chocolate and coffee over medium heat, stirring until smooth.

2. Add sugar and cook 5 minutes more.

3. Stir in butter, vanilla, and optional liqueur.

4. Pour hot sauce over ice cream to harden.

This can be stored in a jar and refrigerated. Uncover and heat up the jar of sauce in a pan of water.

COOKING TIME: 10 minutes

STRAWBERRIES WITH LEMON CREAM

We had lots of strawberries at Uphill. My favorites were the tiny woodland berries, frais de bois, sun-warmed and too tiny for much else than juicy eating on the spot. This simple dessert has become a tradition on our annual 4th of July picnic. Garnish with strawberries from the garden and notice how quickly they disappear. Be sure to pack extra berries for dipping!

2 cups whipping cream

1/2 cup granulated sugar

4 lemons, the juice and grated zest

2 tablespoons condensed milk

GARNISH

Strawberries, blueberries, and raspberries

1. Combine all ingredients in a large, chilled mixing bowl.

2. Beat until very thick.

3. Divide among glasses or heap into a bowl.

4. Chill until serving. Garnish with berries.

YIELD: 8 servings

PREPARATION TIME: 10 minutes

VARIATIONS: Change fruit garnishes according to the freshest available: raspberries, blueberries, blackberries, etc. Fill bottom of crystal bowl with berries and then heap on lemon cream and garnish. Delicious also as a filling in a meringue pie crust shell. Use light cream for a lighter, lower-fat touch.

COUNTRY BAKED APPLES

In the orchard were some old, unidentified apple trees. Many of these varieties baked particularly well — both keeping their shape and having nice flavor. Serve this dessert with softly whipped cream alongside.

2 baking apples, Rome beauty or Cortland

Lemon juice

Whipping cream, (whipped with confectioners' sugar, if desired)

FILLING #1

2 tablespoons butter or margarine

3 tablespoons brown sugar

1 teaspoon cinnamon

$1/3$ cup oats

2 tablespoons butter or margarine, reserve

FILLING #2

3 tablespoons good apricot preserves

$1/4$ teaspoon lemon peel

1 tablespoon calvados or brandy

1 tablespoon sliced almonds

2 tablespoons butter or margarine, reserve

1. Preheat oven to 400 degrees.

2. Wash and dry apples. Peel $1/3$ of the way down the apple. Core from the stem end, being careful not to pierce through the bottom. A spoon can be used to dig out and increase the cavity size.

3. Rub a small amount of lemon juice over cut surfaces to prevent discoloration.

4. Combine filling ingredients for filling #1 or #2, reserving last 2 tablespoons butter in each recipe.

5. Spoon prepared filling inside each apple.

6. Place apples in an ovenproof dish. Divide butter; place on top of the apples.

7. Fill dish with water to 1" deep. Bake uncovered for 45 minutes or until tender.

8. Serve each apple on an individual plate. Pass a pitcher of heavy cream or softly whipped cream flavored with calvados and confectioners' sugar.

YIELD: Enough filling for 2 apples

PREPARATION TIME: 15 minutes

BAKING TIME: 45 minutes

VARIATION: Wrap baked apples in squares of puff pastry and bake, as directed. Add raisins to the filling for a flavorful change.

Pumpkin Bread Pudding with Whiskey Hard Sauce

Dark and delicious, this pudding is made after Thanksgiving with any leftover pumpkin bread (see page 25). We've also made the bread just to have the pudding. It's habit-forming!

1 tablespoon butter

1/2 loaf plus 2 slices pumpkin bread (see page 25)

3 cups warm milk

3 eggs

5 tablespoons granulated sugar

1 teaspoon vanilla extract

1/2 teaspoon almond extract

1. Preheat oven to 350 degrees.

2. Spread 1 tablespoon butter in a casserole dish.

3. Set aside 2 slices of bread. Slice the 1/2 loaf into approximately 1/3" slices. Stack these and cut into about 3/4" fingers. There should be about 4 cups, packed loosely. Reserve.

4. In a saucepan, heat the milk. Toss with the bread pieces. Let sit for 15 minutes.

5. In a separate bowl, combine eggs, 4 tablespoons sugar, and extracts. Beat well.

6. Combine bread and eggs together in the casserole. Stir all together with a wooden spoon.

7. Cut the remaining 2 slices of bread into quarters. Lay on top of pudding. Sprinkle with remaining 1 tablespoon sugar.

8. Bake for 1 hour or longer until a knife inserted comes out almost clean.

9. Spoon into small bowls. Add a spoonful of Whiskey Hard Sauce to top.

YIELD: 8–10 servings
PREPARATION TIME: 20 minutes
BAKING TIME: 60–70 minutes

WHISKEY HARD SAUCE

4 tablespoons butter, room temperature

1 cup confectioners' sugar

1 1/2 teaspoons bourbon or whiskey

1 teaspoon light cream, optional

1. Cream the butter.

2. Gradually add the confectioners' sugar, continuing to cream until fluffy.

3. Stir in whiskey and cream.

4. Spread on a small plate in a mound about 1" high. Refrigerate.

YIELD: About 1/2 cup
PREPARATION TIME: 10 minutes
VARIATION: The hard sauce can be flavored with vanilla extract, orange rind and juice, or rum.

MOTHER'S RICE PUDDING

Rumor has it you need my mother's big yellow bowl to make this creamy rice pudding taste just right, but I'm convinced any bowl will do. I've learned to test rice pudding and custards by sticking a knife in near the edge, not near the center. When it comes out clean, the pudding is done.

4 cups milk

$2/3$–1 cup granulated sugar

1 tablespoon vanilla extract

$1/2$ cup raisins

$1/3$–$1/2$ cup cooked rice (I use brown rice)

5 eggs, beaten

1. Preheat oven to 325 degrees.

2. Combine all of the ingredients in a medium-sized ovenproof serving bowl or casserole.

3. To bake, set bowl in a pan of water.

4. Bake for about 1 hour and 10 minutes, or until a knife inserted near edge comes out clean.

YIELD: 8–10 servings
PREPARATION TIME: 15 minutes
BAKING TIME: 75 minutes

Wild Farm Maple Cottage Pudding

This recipe was printed on the maple syrup labels at Wild Farm. It is an old recipe, a homey farm dish that still tastes delicious.

1 cup maple syrup

3 tablespoons sugar

3 tablespoons butter

1 egg

1/2 cup milk

1 cup flour

1 1/2 teaspoons baking powder

1/4 teaspoon salt

Chopped nuts, optional

1. Preheat oven to 350 degrees.

2. Heat the syrup to boiling point.

3. Pour in a 8" x 8" pan.

4. Mix sugar, butter, egg, and milk. Beat well.

5. Sift flour with baking powder and salt. Add to the batter; stir.

6. Pour batter over hot syrup. Bake for 25–30 minutes.

7. Turn out of pan and sprinkle with nuts.

YIELD: 8 servings

PREPARATION TIME: 10 minutes

COOKING TIME: 30 minutes

TOBLERONE™ FONDUE

We are quite a group of homebodies, favoring a houseful of friends who are spirited game players to nights out and about. This is particularly true on New Year's Eve. On this night, we have a bonfire out back, where we dance, cheer, and make toasts to welcome the new year. We have this fondue at midnight.

Three 3-ounce bars of Toblerone™ chocolate

1/2 cup heavy cream

1–2 tablespoons liqueur (Grand Marnier, kirsch, or rum), optional

1. Separate chocolate into triangles, and melt with the cream in the top of a double boiler.

2. Add optional liqueur.

3. Pour into a fondue pot and keep warm over a candle.

4. Serve with fruit and plain cakes for dipping.

YIELD: 6 servings
PREPARATION TIME: 5 minutes

HOLIDAY FLORENTINES

These cookies are delicious just as they are, or with chocolate sides sandwiched together with mocha butter cream. Stack them in clear bags and tie with gold ribbons. They make lovely and delicious gifts.

1/2 cup light cream

1/4 cup sugar

1/4 cup corn syrup

1 teaspoon dried orange chopped

1/3 cup almonds, finely chopped

1/4 cup flour

6 ounces semisweet chocolate bits

1. Preheat oven to 350 degrees.

2. Combine cream, sugar, corn syrup, and bring to a boil.

3. Cook to 238 degrees (testing with candy thermometer), then take off heat.

4. Stir in rind, almonds, and flour.

5. Drop by teaspoonfuls onto a buttered cookie sheet. Flatten.

6. Bake 8–10 minutes until golden and lacy.

7. Cool 1 minute and transfer to a wire rack.

8. Melt chocolate bits in the top of a double boiler.

9. Brush a thin layer of chocolate over the smooth sides of cookies. Allow to dry.

YIELD: 4 dozen cookies
PREPARATION TIME: 10 minutes
COOKING TIME: 10 minutes

FROSTED BROWN COW COOKIES

Each Christmas I spend an entire evening frosting cookies — not trees or sprinkled stars, but my favorite — cow-shaped cookies. I use cocoa-flavored icing for the brown spots. They look great in baskets filled with dried grass or hay. We deliver them to neighbors on Christmas Eve day.

Be sure to decorate them, as plain cookies are only half the fun.

COOKIES

1/2 cup butter

2/3 cup granulated sugar

1 egg

1 tablespoon orange juice

1–2 teaspoons grated lemon rind

2 1/2 cups flour

1 teaspoon baking powder

1/4 teaspoon salt

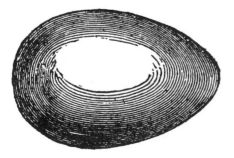

COOKIES:

1. Cream butter and sugar in a large bowl until light and fluffy.

2. Beat in egg, orange juice, and lemon rind.

3. Sift together dry ingredients.

4. Gradually stir dry ingredients into creamed mixture.

5. Gather the dough into a ball and wrap in plastic wrap. Refrigerate several hours or overnight.

6. Preheat oven to 350 degrees.

7. Roll out half of the dough on a lightly floured surface to 1/8" thickness. Cut with a cookie cutter that has first been dipped in flour.

8. Place cookies on lightly greased baking sheets. Repeat until all dough is used.

9. Bake a single sheet at a time for 8 minutes or until the edges are just lightly browned. The cookies should remain pale.

10. Remove cookies from sheet and cool on wire rack.

FROSTING

2 egg whites

2 1/2 – 3 cups confectioners' sugar

1 tablespoon milk

Cocoa

FROSTING:

1. Beat egg whites until foamy.

2. Gradually add sugar, beating until thick and creamy.

3. Add tablespoon of milk. Reserve some white frosting. Separate some to color with the cocoa. Decorate cookies with brown spots.

YIELD: Approximately 3 dozen
PREPARATION TIME: 30 minutes
COOKING TIME: 8 minutes per batch

INDEX

D

E

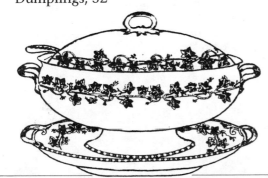

R

S

More good books from
WILLIAMSON PUBLISHING

To order additional copies of **Country Suppers from Uphill Farm**, please enclose $10.95 per copy plus $2.50 shipping and handling. Follow "To Order" instructions on the last page. Thank you.

DINING ON DECK: Fine Foods for Sailing and Boating
by Linda Vail

Savor the moment...casual elegance and fine foods with minimal effort! More than 200 recipes for breakfasts, lunches, dinners plus 90 menus for day sails, elegant week-ends, onboard brunches, and hearty suppers. Plenty of tips on provisioning and storage, too.

160 pages, 8 x 10, illustrations
Quality paperback, $10.95

THE BROWN BAG COOKBOOK: Nutritious Portable Lunches for Kids and Grown-Ups
by Sara Sloan

Now in its eleventh printing this popular book has more than 1,000 brown bag lunch ideas with 150 recipes for simple, quick, nutritious lunches that kids will love. Breakfast ideas, too! The more people care what they eat, the more popular this book becomes.

192 pages, 8¼ x 7¼, illustrations
Quality paperback, $9.95

GOLDE'S HOMEMADE COOKIES
by Golde Soloway

Over 50,000 copies of this marvelous cookbook have been sold. Now its in its second edition with 135 of the most delicious cookie recipes imaginable. *Publishers Weekly* says, "Cookies are her chosen realm and how sweet a world it is to visit." You're sure to agree!

176 pages, 8¼ x 7¼, illustrations
Quality paperback, $8.95

KIDS COOK! Fabulous Food For The Whole Family
by Sarah Williamson and Zachary Williamson

Here's a cookbook written for kids by two teenagers who know what kids like to eat! *Kids Cook!* is filled with over 150 recipes for great tasting foods that kids ages 8 and up can cook for themselves and for their families and friends, too. Try breakfast bonanzas like *Breakfast Sundaes*, great lunches including *Chicken Shirt Pocket*, super salads like *A Whale of a Fruit Salad*, quick snacks and easy extras like *Nacho Nibbles*, delicious dinners including *Pizza Originale*, and dynamite desserts and soda fountain treats including *Chocolate Surprise Cupcakes*. All recipes are for "real," healthy foods — not cutesy recipes that are no fun to eat. Plus Nutri Notes, Safety First, and plenty of special menus for Father's Day, Grandma's Teatime, picnics, and parties. One terrific book!

176 pages, 11 x 8½, Over 150 recipes, illustrations
Quality paperback, $12.95

Easy-to-Make TEDDY BEARS & All The Trimmings
by Jodie Davis

Now you can make the most lovable, huggable, plain or fancy teddy bears imaginable, for a fraction of store-bought costs. Step-by-step instructions and easy patterns drawn to actual size for large, soft-bodied bears, quilted bears, and even jointed bears. Plus patterns for clothes, accessories—even teddy bear furniture!

208 pages, 8½ x 11, illustrations and patterns
Quality paperback, $13.95

Easy-To-Make CLOTH DOLLS & All The Trimmings
by Jodie Davis

Jodie Davis turns her many talents to making the most adorable and personable cloth dolls imaginable. With her expert directions and clear full-sized patterns, anyone can create these instant friends for a special child or friend. Includes seven 18-inch dolls like Santa, Raggedy Ann, and a clown; a 20-inch baby doll plus complete wardrobe; a 25-inch boy and girl doll plus a wardrobe including sailor suits; and 10 dolls from around the world including a Japanese kimono doll and Amish dolls. Absolutely beautiful and you can do it!

224 pages, 8½ x 11, illustrations and patterns
Quality paperback, $13.95

Easy-To-Make STUFFED ANIMALS & All The Trimmings
by Jodie Davis

With Jodie Davis's complete and easy instructions, creating adorable stuffed animals has never been easier. Whether you are making gifts for children or additions for a special doll collection, these fuzzy animals are sure to delight anyone. Includes 14-inch unicorn, Rudolph doll, and a large assortment of farm animals — complete with clothing patterns!

208 pages, 8½ x 11, illustrations and patterns
Quality paperback, $13.95

· ·

To Order:

At your bookstore or order directly from Williamson Publishing. We accept Visa and MasterCard (please include number and expiration date), or send check to:

Williamson Publishing Company
Church Hill Road, P.O. Box 185
Charlotte, Vermont 05445

Toll-free phone orders with credit cards:

1-800-234-8791

Please add $2.50 per total order for postage and handling. Satisfaction is guaranteed or full refund without questions or quibbles.